HEAVEN CHANGES EVERYTHING

HEAVEN CHANGES EVERYTHING

LIVING EVERY DAY
with ETERNITY *in* MIND

TODD AND SONJA BURPO

THOMAS NELSON
Since 1798

NASHVILLE   DALLAS   MEXICO CITY   RIO DE JANEIRO

Published in Nashville, Tennessee, by Thomas Nelson. Thomas Nelson is a registered trademark of Thomas Nelson, Inc.

The author is represented by the literary agency of Alive Communications, Inc., 7680 Goddard Street, Suite 200, Colorado Springs, Colorado 80920, www.alivecommunications.com.

Thomas Nelson, Inc. titles may be purchased in bulk for educational, business, fund-raising, or sales promotional use. For information, please e-mail *SpecialMarkets@ThomasNelson.com*.

Unless otherwise noted, Scripture quotations are taken from the New King James Version. © 1982 by Thomas Nelson, Inc. Used by permission. All rights reserved.

Other Scripture references are from the following sources: The King James Version (KJV). *The Message* (MSG) by Eugene H. Peterson. © 1993, 1994,1995, 1996, 2000, 2001, 2002. Used by permission of NavPress Publishing Group. All rights reserved. The New CenturyVersion (NCV). © 2005 by Thomas Nelson, Inc. Used by permission. All rights reserved. The Holy Bible, New International Version (NIV). © 1973, 1978, 1984, 2011 by Biblica Inc. Used by permission of Zondervan. All rights reserved worldwide.

Some names and details in stories and anecdotes have been changed to protect identities.

Library of Congress Cataloging-in-Publication Data

Burpo, Todd.
  Heaven changes everything : living every day with eternity in mind / Todd and Sonja Burpo.
    p. cm.
  ISBN 978-0-8499-4841-1
1. Christian life. 2. Burpo, Todd. Heaven is for real. 3. Heaven--Christianity. 4. Near-death experiences--Religious aspects--Christianity. I. Burpo, Sonja. II. Title.
  BV4501.3.B8735 2012
  248.4--dc23

                                    2012030259

Printed in the United States of America
12 13 14 15 16 QG 7 6 5 4 3

*We've been given a brand-new life
and have everything to live for,
including a future in heaven—and
the future starts now!*

—1 Peter 1:5 msg

To parents who have lost children, born
and unborn, may you find the
comfort of heaven your child has found.

To all who are missing loved ones, may you find the
assurance of the reunion awaiting you in heaven.

To the tired and sometimes forgotten
children's workers, may you hear
the applause coming from the throne of heaven.

To those who have been wounded
and rejected, may you find
the healing and love that the Lord of
heaven offers you here and now.

And to anyone who is still uncertain
about heaven, may you discover
that God's incredible gift is real and
that you can receive it today.

CONTENTS

We Interrupt This Program . . .

In the passenger seat, Sonja turned so that she could see our son, whose car seat was parked behind mine. I pictured his blond crew cut and his sky-blue eyes shining in the dark. "Do you remember the hospital, Colton?" Sonja said.

"Yes, Mommy, I remember," he said. "That's where the angels sang to me."

—*Heaven Is for Real, XVII*

Have you ever been watching a television show or listening to the radio and suddenly a voice says something like, "We interrupt this program for an important message from XYZ News"? If you're familiar with that kind of interruption, you understand how the story we shared in *Heaven Is for Real* unfolded for us. Again and again our young son interrupted our lives with little strings of words that stopped us in our tracks:

"That's where the angels sang to me."

Or . . .

"I was sitting on Jesus' lap."

Or . . .

"You had a baby die in your tummy, didn't you?"

Hearing these statements, we wondered, *How did you know that?*

In casual, little-boy language, Colton would mention something that had happened to him in heaven or something he had learned there. These little interruptions became life-changers for us as we realized his story was true and that it held huge implications for our lives—and for others'. We began to let God teach us through our son.

In addition to writing Colton's story in *Heaven Is for Real,* we began sharing our experience with audiences around the country. Along the way, we encountered more "interruptions" of memorable moments and life lessons as people shared their own stories or responded with new insights that reinforced what God was teaching us about heaven.

We've written this book to share those new "interruptions" and insights that came to us either through an idea God sparked in our hearts or through people who shared their own story in response to ours. Each one is drawn from one of Colton's "interruptions" or from some other part of his astounding story shared in *Heaven Is for Real.* Some chapters will be short, others longer; like most interruptions, their length and impact are unpredictable. Put together, they reveal how our experience continues to show how heaven changes everything about our life here on earth.

We understand now that Colton's little-boy descriptions of heaven that interrupted our days were actually God's interruptions of our lives. He nudged us unexpectedly with moments that made us gasp—and then grasp the truth, again, that heaven is for real.

We pray that the thoughts and lessons we share here will interrupt your life with heavenly perspective the way they interrupted ours and that living every day with eternity in mind will change everything for you too.

—Todd and Sonja Burpo
June 2012

ONE

ONE

Heaven—We're Not There Yet

For my family, the July Fourth weekend of 2003 was a big deal. . . . My wife, Sonja, and I had planned to take the kids to visit Sonja's brother, Steve, and his family in Sioux Falls, South Dakota. . . . It would be our first chance to meet our nephew, Bennett, born two months earlier. . . . This trip would be the first time we'd left our hometown of Imperial, Nebraska, since a family trip to Greeley, Colorado, in March had turned into the worst nightmare of our lives.

To put it bluntly, the last time we had taken a family trip, one of our children almost died. Call us crazy, but we were a little apprehensive this time, almost to the point of not wanting to go. Now, as a pastor, I'm not a believer in superstition. Still, some weird, unsettled part of me felt that if we just hunkered down close to home, we'd be safe.

—*Heaven Is for Real, xv–xvi*

Todd

Maybe you're like me and wonder sometimes, as your feet hit the floor, *Is this going to be a good day or a bad day?* Wouldn't we all like to know the answer to that question? Then we could just stay in bed some mornings and avoid the calamity awaiting us.

Maybe, like me, you've gone through some kind of gut-wrenching experience or some heartbreaking loss that makes you apprehensive as you begin each day now. Enduring a life-altering trauma can make you want to play the turtle and go inside your shell.

After seventeen days of watching my toddler suffer, I'd managed only about five nights of sleep. My life had been so painful during that time and I had been wounded so deeply that it took almost four months after Colton's hospitalization before I could really function again. There was no doubt that my faith in God—and even more, my faith in myself—had been stretched to the limits. The last thing on my to-do list was to repeat anything like I'd just endured.

But you have to go on living. You have to get out of bed in the morning. The question is, *how?*

Jesus said in this world we're going to have trouble. (Do I hear a big "Amen!" out there?) He spent time here on earth and endured the worst trouble anyone could imagine. So he knows better than anyone that this isn't heaven. But he also knows there's a place where there's no suffering and no trouble, and he's inviting us to join him there.

Today, people are looking for peace in the midst of trouble. But peace is an elusive thing. Looking for peace in worldly sources, many people become addicted to drugs or sex or other harmful substances or behaviors. Then

Jesus comes along and makes this incredible claim: *If you trust me, I will give you peace.* One way we gain that peace is by believing his promise that, no matter how bad things get here on earth, we're headed for a better place: heaven.

Where do *you* find peace? How about looking for it in the Creator of the universe? In the One who said, "Yeah, in *this* world, you're gonna have trouble. But you can relax. I've overcome all that stuff. I'll help you get through it. And then someday I'll take you back to my place, where life's hurts don't exist. I know things are bad now, but heaven's ahead. And you're gonna love it."

> *How would you live your life differently today if you knew, without a doubt, that no matter what happens, everything is going to be okay, even wonderful, in the end?*

> *In this world you will have trouble. But take heart! I have overcome the world.*
>
> —John 16:33 NIV

TWO

Missing the Miracles

I noticed we were passing through the traffic light where, if we turned left, we'd wind up at the Great Plains Regional Medical Center. That was where we'd spent fifteen night- marish days in March, much of it on our knees, praying for God to spare Colton's life. . . .

Sometimes laughter is the only way to process tough times, so as we passed the turnoff, I decided to rib Colton a little.

"Hey, Colton, if we turn here, we can go back to the hospital," I said. "Do you wanna go back to the hospital?"

—HEAVEN IS FOR REAL, XVII

Todd

God is sovereign. The way he orchestrates the tiniest details in our lives to carry out his will for us is simply beyond our understanding. I believe God is involved in every part of our lives, in small decisions and in monumental matters.

Consider this one: late one night, on a long cross-country

drive to visit relatives, I jokingly asked our four-year-old son if he wanted to go back to the hospital where he had almost died a few months earlier. His casual answer would change our lives forever. Talking about the hospital, Colton told Sonja and me, "That's where the angels sang to me."

Over the next few weeks and months, other details of Colton's miraculous visit to heaven gradually trickled out. But if I hadn't asked that question that night, who knows when—or if—we would ever have known about it.

God is constantly at work in our lives in ways that we might not even realize.

Consider this: God's Son's first recorded miracle occurred when he attended a big wedding party where the wine ran out. Jesus instructed the servants to fill the containers with water, and then he turned that water into wine. One thing a lot of people miss in that story is that the bridegroom and bride didn't know they had run out of wine. In fact, they *never* knew! So they never knew that Jesus had turned the water into wine. God did a miracle for this couple, and they didn't even know he'd done it.

It makes me wonder, how many miracles has God done for us and we didn't even know he was at work? How many times has God directed us to turn left or turn right at an intersection and that turn kept us from an accident or brought us to encounter someone at exactly the right time so we could help or encourage him or her at exactly the right moment? How many times has he prompted us to reach out to someone, to ask a question that made a difference, and we didn't recognize his hand at work in that moment?

We don't often have problems bringing the *big* stuff to God, but remember, there is nothing too small for God to be involved with in our lives—whether or not we realize it at the time.

> **When's the last time you noticed God at work in your life? If you need a little help, listen to George Strait's song "I Saw God Today."**

The master of the banquet tasted the water that had been turned into wine. He did not realize where it had come from, though the servants who had drawn the water knew.

—John 2:9 NIV

THREE

Watching for God-cidents

Inside the Expedition, time froze. Sonja and I looked at each other, passing a silent message: Did he just say what I think he said?

Sonja leaned over and whispered, "Has he talked to you about angels before?"

I shook my head no. "You?"

She shook her head.

—HEAVEN IS FOR REAL, XVIII

Sonja

Colton interrupted our days with glimpses of heaven shared in bits of conversation I call "shock and awe."

For example, he would make some casual comment, like telling Todd that Todd's grandpa, Pop, who died in 1975, "has really big wings."

Or like telling me, "Jesus shoots down power for Daddy when he's talking."

Or describing an incident that happened to Todd when he was thirteen that Todd had never shared with our kids.

Colton kept telling Todd and me things he could not have known except by firsthand experience or someone telling him. And absolutely we knew that no one on this planet had told him! Remember, he was just turning four years old. And each time he dropped one of these little shock-and-awe bombs on us, Todd and I would have the same conversation:

"How did he know that? Did *you* tell him?"

"No, did you?"

"No."

Then there would be a moment of silence as we gave each other the same perplexed look.

Colton told us personal things that had happened in our lives long before he was born. If there had been an autobiography of the Burpo family at that time, Colton would have described most of the turning points in it. If we didn't know or remember it ourselves, we would ask others, like Todd's mom, who would say, "Yes, we *did* do that," or, "Yes, that *did* happen."

And Colton told us things about heaven—like the fact that Jesus's chair in heaven "is right next to his Dad's." When Todd asked which side, Colton was clear to point out that Jesus sat on God's *right* side.

We confirmed everything that could be confirmed either in the Bible or from someone's personal memory. And we got to the point where we learned to listen to Colton more closely. We knew his experience was real and that something spectacular had happened. We knew what he'd said was accurate, so we were constantly tuned in, wondering what was coming next. If there was no earthly explanation for what Colton told us, we knew there had to be a heavenly one.

The one thing we *didn't* have to confirm was that God was involved. We knew that without question.

What about you? Has something happened in your life that could have no earthly explanation? Did a stranger say something to you in the checkout line that was just the right word of encouragement you needed at the end of a long, stressful day? Was it a "coincidence" that you ran into someone at the post office and, without thinking, you said just the words *she* needed to hear? Did you have a dream that gave you a new perspective on a difficult situation? Did your child say or do something amazing that took your breath away?

Other people might call these unexplainable events *coincidences*. But did you know the word *coincidence* is not found in the Bible? Instead I use my own word when I'm thinking about these experiences. If your mind is open to the fact that heaven is real and you can go there someday, you may want to adopt my word into your vocabulary too.

I call them *God*-cidents.

What gift has God sent your way recently that you dismissed as a coincidence?

When he was at the table with them, he took bread, gave thanks, broke it and began to give it to them. Then their eyes were opened and they recognized him.

—Luke 24:30–31 NIV

FOUR

Solving the Puzzle

As I stood there and thought through a scriptural basis for experiencing heaven without dying, I realized that Colton, in telling me he had died "for a little bit," had only been trying to match up his pastor-dad's assertion with what he knew to be the facts of his own experience. Kind of like walking outside and finding that the street is wet, and concluding, well, okay, it must have rained.

—HEAVEN IS FOR REAL, 80–81

Todd

The only time I work jigsaw puzzles is when I'm coerced, usually by one of my kids. Then the only way out of it is to just get the thing done, which for me means looking at the picture on the top of the box. Yes, I know there are ways to put it together without looking at the picture—you can pull out the edge pieces or sort out the colors. But I'm one of those guys who isn't big on following directions. I *am* good at looking at pictures. Just show me the picture, and let's get on with it.

In many ways, Bible verses about heaven are like pieces of a jigsaw puzzle, but the problem is that the Bible doesn't have a picture of heaven on the cover. How do you put the pieces together without a picture? Reading some of those Scripture verses is like sitting down at the puzzle table and looking at a big pile of pieces with no clue how they go together. It's hard. Confusing. Frustrating.

And then along comes a kid, Colton, telling us he's been to heaven and here's what it's like. He describes his visit to heaven in the words of a young child, words that everyone can understand. Colton's story helps create the picture we need so we can see how the puzzle pieces about heaven fit together.

Stories help us understand lots of complicated things. Jesus used many stories about everyday things—farmers, fig trees, sheep, wolves and shepherds, fishermen—so that anyone listening could understand the truth behind those stories.

A lot of people have a hope of heaven, but they're kind of sketchy on the pieces of the puzzle and how they fit together. Some of the Bible's passages about heaven are hard to understand. For many people, Colton's visit to heaven, told in our simple story, provides that "aha!" moment when suddenly the picture comes together.

Once we can "see" heaven and understand that it's *real,* all sorts of good things happen to us in personal, every-day ways. Doubts are removed. Endurance is strengthened. Courage is emboldened. Grief is erased. It's like a little kid is saying earnestly to all of us, "Jesus is the truth, and he can be trusted."

And we believe him.

At least, that's how it has worked for me. And other people have let me know Colton's experience helped them the same way. One of them is my mom. She told me, "Ever since this happened, I think more about what it might really be like in heaven. I accepted the idea of heaven before, but now I visualize it. Before, I'd heard, but now I know that someday I'm going to see."

If you've pushed the Bible's puzzle pieces to the corner of your life because the puzzle just seems too hard to figure out, let Colton's story provide the picture you need to see how the pieces fit together.

For some earthly practice in putting together the Bible's words about heaven, Sonja suggests sitting down with your kids and working a jigsaw puzzle. (Todd says look at the picture first. You'll get finished faster.)

He taught by using stories, many stories. . . . He continued, "Do you see how this story works? All my stories work this way."

—MARK 4:2, 13 MSG

FIVE

Call Your Dad!

The sound of my leg breaking was so loud that I imagined the ball had zinged in from the outfield and smacked it. Fire exploded in my shin and ankle. I fell to my back, contracted into a fetal position, and pulled my knee up to my belly.

—*HEAVEN IS FOR REAL*, 8

Todd

Life was good for the Burpos. Sonja and I had two healthy children, a comfortable home, and jobs we enjoyed. Sonja was a schoolteacher, and I pastored a small but growing church in a town we were happy to call home.

Then, in a coed softball tournament, I slid down the baseline while stealing third base and broke my leg—and also snapped the bones in my ankle in two different places.

While my pastoring work and Sonja's job with the school brought in some money, our primary source of income was the garage door company I owned. But it's pretty hard to climb ladders to install garage doors with a knee that won't bend while you're wearing a heavy cast the length of your leg. No surprise, our bank balance took a sudden and rapid nosedive.

While recovering from the broken leg and the plunging finances, I was hit with a severe attack of kidney stones. Right after that, I was diagnosed with the precursor to—get this—breast cancer. *Hyperplasia* was the word the doctor used.

Other pastors in our district started calling me "Pastor Job" after the Bible character who was struck with a series of increasingly severe setbacks. Like Job, I struggled to deal with life as one crisis after another struck my family.

Then, just as my own health problems were resolving, Colton suffered the ruptured appendix that almost killed him.

What we learned during those challenges was that we learn more during challenges than while life is good!

One thing I noticed was that, in the middle of all those problems, I was never too busy to pray. Isn't it amazing that in the midst of our problems we seem to have plenty of time to pray, but when things are going smoothly we are often "too busy"?

Here I was a pastor, someone who had prayer ingrained into every part of my life, yet it was my problems that caused my prayer time to increase and become more fervent. I'd often noticed how people never took the time to pray until they had a problem—and now I was noticing that my problems were having that same effect on my life too.

As a pastor, I pray a lot. But during that time I realized that I *could* pray a lot more—because I did.

The only time God even shows up on some people's radar is when they're in the midst of a crisis. It's like the situation some parents of college kids have with their children: they don't hear from the kids except when they need money. Aren't we the perfect example of that ourselves with our heavenly Father? He only hears from us when we need help.

If we take time to think about it, we realize that not only do we grow as people when we go through hard times but our understanding of God grows at the same time. Many people wander away during the good times and stray from God. But when hard times hit, they come running back to him. How much better it is if we stay close to God through the bad times *and* the good.

I remember a young man, I'll call him John, who came to me a few years ago, very upset because of what his family was going through. One family member had been found guilty of abusing his wife, another had been arrested for stealing, and another arrested for doing drugs. This man asked angrily, "Why does God let this happen to my family?"

He must have caught me in bad mood, because I wasn't having any of it that day. I said, "John, how can you lie like that?"

He was stunned. "What do you mean? It's the truth," he insisted.

I said, "You're asking me why God lets this happen. Well, let me ask you something: which person in your family is living for God? Which person in your family has Jesus in his heart? Which one is trying to follow Christ?"

John's demeanor changed. He dropped his head and said very slowly but honestly, "None of us."

"So how can you blame God for your problems?" I asked. "It sounds to me like all the trouble you're telling me about is because God is not there—yet you're blaming him for what you did to yourselves? How can you do that?"

John got my point, and he took my words to heart. The next day, he made a change and committed to put Jesus first in his life.

I'd like to say John's family's situation immediately changed for the better, but of course that's not what happened. Still, it was a starting point, and I have no doubt that John is having a strong impact on his family as they see the change that's happening in *him*.

It's a lesson we all can learn right now. (It turns out you don't *have* to be going through a challenging time to learn something!) If we put God front and center in our lives, if we give him more attention throughout each and every day, we may just find that the challenging times, when they come, are a little less challenging.

Maybe this moment—*right now*—is a good time for you to think about what God has done for you. Maybe you can change your priorities. Maybe instead of only praying when you're in trouble you can resolve to "phone home" to heaven more often and say, "Thank you, Father" instead of only calling when you're in trouble and begging, "God, help me!"

Just like parents of college kids want to hear from their kids when they don't need money, God likes to hear from us when we don't need something. When was the last time you prayed only to "check in" with God and say, "Thanks, Dad"?

Since everything here today might well be gone tomorrow, do you see how essential it is to live a holy life? Daily expect the Day of God, eager for its arrival. The galaxies will burn up and the elements melt down that day—but we'll hardly notice. We'll be looking the other way, ready for the promised new heavens and the promised new earth, all landscaped with righteousness.

—2 PETER 3:11–13 MSG

SIX

Acquiring a Heavenly Perspective

I . . . began working my way upstairs on my crutches. Down at the bottom, on the first step, I started getting mad at God.

"This isn't fair," I grumbled aloud as I struggled up the stairs, one crutch at a time, one step at a time. "I have to suffer and be in this pathetic state for them to give me the help I've needed all along."

Feeling pretty smug in my martyrdom, I had just reached the top landing when a still, small voice arose in my heart: And what did my Son do for you?

—HEAVEN IS FOR REAL, 12

Todd

It's fun to watch babies learn to walk. Parents are quick to videotape and count the number of steps their little ones take—until they fall, that is. The little ones, usually determined, get up and try again—and fall again. What do parents do then? They don't scold, they don't run away, they don't duck their heads in shame as their children are learning to walk. Instead, they encourage and cheer each awkward step, and they reach down and set their kids back on their feet when they fall so they can try to walk again.

What is that? Do you call it love? Do you call it patience? Is it healthy parenting? I think it's a great example of a different perspective, one that's filled with *grace*.

This perspective is based in reality. Parents know their toddlers are going to fall. But they also have confidence that their children will eventually learn to walk because the odds say so. The parents learned to walk as toddlers. Big brother and sister eventually learned to walk. The neighbor's kids did. And most likely the next little one will conquer walking as well.

Now consider this: Where does our heavenly Father find his perspective as he watches his children—you and me—in our daily walk? Does he trust in the odds, personal experience, or something far greater?

God's wisdom about your life can come from many places. Heaven gives him an unequaled vantage point. First, he made you. Like an engineer understands a car he or she designed, no one understands your limitations and possibilities better than the God who created you.

Second, God has incomprehensible experience. What type of degree do you earn for helping people of all generations learn to walk through the difficulties and challenges of this world?

Third, God is not surprised by your tomorrows. Nobody else, even the best loving parent, can look into your future and prepare you for what lies ahead and how to overcome it. He knows you're going to struggle, make mistakes, and fail. But he also knows you're surrounded by his gifts of forgiveness and grace.

So what can that type of perspective do for you? Well, speaking personally, it keeps me from getting off track. My life seems to be a constant battle of making choices. I want to be a good provider for my family, a loving husband for my wife, an involved parent for my children, and the right example for my congregation. But I constantly deal with obstacles like exhaustion, confusion, selfishness, lack of resources, and ultimately, lack of focus. When I get bogged down with these struggles, I tend to drift off course.

Fall 2002 was one of those extreme periods in my life. I had been swamped with a load of additional health challenges, and I could feel my boat not just drifting but sinking fast.

As a result, this small-town pastor threw himself a big pity party one day as he struggled up the church stairs on crutches, complaining and whining all the way.

With every step I managed to climb, I voiced one more justified complaint to God. I was rehearsing in my mind all the sacrifices I had made and was questioning my lack of reward. It was such a strange moment. As my body rose up the stairwell, my spirit was sinking further into a pit.

When I reached the landing, something happened that helped my spirit join the rest of my body. God spoke.

No, he didn't send a bolt of lightning to correct my attitude. Instead, I sensed a voice speaking gently into my heart, asking, *And what did my Son do for you?*

Boy, that's just like God! With just one small question, he can change your entire perspective. With that one reminder, all the selfishness I was struggling with was replaced by a mountain of gratefulness as I remembered the gift of grace I'd been given.

Some people don't get to experience grace, though. They're afraid to turn to God when life gets hard and they make mistakes and fall from their Christian walk. They expect to be ridiculed, condemned, or scolded. They're trying to avoid the heavenly "I told you so" they anticipate rumbling down from the throne of God.

But that's not what happens.

I'm not the only one who's found that God speaks in a still, small, yet comforting voice when I fall. Elijah was a prophet in the Old Testament who thought life had become unfair. He felt like he was alone, without support; he was fed up and he was giving up. His words to God were, "Let me die." (1 Kings 19:4 NCV).

Fortunately for Elijah, God had other plans. The Bible says God came to Elijah. But he didn't speak to him roughly. He spoke to him in a still, small voice, just like he did for me.

I hope you've never gotten to that point where Elijah did, wanting to die, but if you have, know that even in the most desperate moments, God wants to talk to you, and he wants to speak words of direction, words of forgiveness, and words of grace into your life.

When you find yourself in that hard place, bitter and discouraged because you've fallen (again), pause for a moment and listen as though God himself were whispering these words into *your* ear: *What did my Son do for you?*

If you can accept that Jesus gave his life for you, as he did for me, consider this wonderful question the apostle Paul asks all of us: Why would God stop there? It makes no sense. Why would grace end at the cross?

The truth is, the cross is the *beginning* of grace. Accepting that truth gives us that all-important heavenly perspective.

You don't see this verse stuck on many refrigerator doors or hung on many church walls, but believe me, it's a verse you need to hide in your heart:

He who did not spare his own Son, but gave him up for us all—how will he not also, along with him, graciously give us all things?
                                        —ROMANS 8:32 NIV

SEVEN

Forgiveness Is for Real

God had blessed me with a small group of believers whom I was charged to shepherd and serve, and here I was griping at God because those believers weren't serving me.

"Lord, forgive me," I said, and swung forward with renewed strength, as if my crutches were eagles' wings.

—*HEAVEN IS FOR REAL, 12–13*

Todd

I've made a few mistakes in my life.

Okay, I've made *a lot* of mistakes. Put that together with my vocation, and you have a pastor who's made a lot of mistakes.

Fortunately, the church I pastor is made up of church members who've made mistakes too. I'm guessing your church is made up of the same kind of people.

You may have heard that pastor's kids aren't perfect either. When something gets broken at our church, the board members joke, "It must have been the pastor's kids."

I give it right back to them and say, "Yes, they were playing with the board members' kids."

Let's face it. We *all* still need grace. We always will.

In *Heaven Is for Real,* I wrote about some of my failures. For example, it was wrong for me to whine to God about the hand I'd been dealt—a broken leg, kidney stones, and a cancer scare—when I'd been given so many blessings: a wonderful wife and children, work that I enjoyed, a comfortable home in a town that I loved, a church filled with good, hard-working believers.

It was also wrong for me to lash out at God with angry words in that closed-off hospital room as my toddler son was undergoing life-and-death surgery down the hall. The reason I feel it was wrong is because I crossed a line. You can be angry and honest with God, and that's okay. But I went beyond that. In the midst of my pain, I was blaming God for some of Satan's attacks against me and my family.

I fell for one of the games Satan plays all the time. He attacks. He hurts. Then he points his crooked finger at God and tries to get us to believe God did it to us. As a thirteen-year-old explained to me, "Satan hurts you. Then he frames God for it."

Closed off in that room I was definitely pleading for intervention, and if I had stopped at that point, it wouldn't have been wrong. But I didn't stop. I fell for Satan's trick. So that episode became one of my very public mistakes, thanks to *Heaven Is for Real.* I don't know if I could write a book long enough to even begin to cover the rest.

But here's the thing: the God who created me knows I'll mess up again. He expects it. And he can handle it.

The Bible is full of stories about believers who made

terrible mistakes, including murder and adultery. Yet when they asked for forgiveness God extended his grace and then used those believers and their mistakes to accomplish mighty things for his kingdom.

Consider the apostle Peter, who made what might be considered the most humiliating mistake of all time. One night as Jesus and the apostles were eating supper, Jesus warned Peter (who was also called Simon) that he was about to make a mistake. He said, "Simon, Simon, Satan has asked to sift all of you as wheat. But I have prayed for you, Simon, that your faith may not fail. And when you have turned back, strengthen your brothers" (Luke 22:31–32 NIV).

Peter was probably shocked by Jesus' words. At that point he did what I've done. He argued with Jesus. Today the dialogue might have gone something like this:

"You're going to fail me, Peter."

"No I'm not."

"Yes you are."

"No I'm not."

"Yes you are."

"No, Jesus. I would *never* do that."

At that point, Jesus must have thought, *Peter, you are so dense.*

But Peter was stubborn. He yelled, "Jesus, I would die for you tonight!"

Oops. Things didn't happen quite the way Peter pictured them. Just a few hours later, Peter fell asleep while supposedly keeping watch in the Garden of Gethsemane. Then, sure enough, after Jesus was arrested and led away by Roman guards, a servant girl in the courtyard recognized Peter and told the others, "This man was with him."

And how did big, bad, bold fisherman Peter respond? He wilted in front of a little girl and denied his Christ. That's pretty embarrassing!

As Satan sifted Peter like wheat, the first of the three denials came out: "Woman, I don't know him," he said.

Peter denied that he knew Jesus two more times that hard night, and no sooner was the third denial out of his mouth than the rooster crowed and Peter realized he had done exactly as the Lord predicted. The Bible says he "wept bitterly" and the weight of his mistake bore down on him (Matt. 26:75)—just like our mistakes bear down on the rest of us when we blow it.

What we don't know but can picture is that while Peter was weeping he probably didn't remember those other words Jesus had said: *I have prayed for you, Simon. . . . And when you have turned back, strengthen your brothers.*

Not *if* you turn back, but *when* you turn back . . .

Probably what Peter missed was that not only did Jesus know Peter was going to fall that night, but he also knew Peter was going to get back up.

The Message version of the Bible paraphrases Jesus' words this way: "Simon, I've prayed for you in particular that you not give in or give out. When you have come through the time of testing, turn to your companions and give them a fresh start."

I hope that *Heaven Is for Real* and *Heaven Changes Everything* will strengthen your faith and give you a fresh start on your road to heaven. That's what Christ's church is all about: helping each other up when we've fallen down.

I remember a few phrases my grandma drilled into my life. One of her favorites was, "Son, if you hit bottom, pick something up while you're down there." Well, this is what I've picked up from those times when I've blown it: God's forgiveness is real, and his grace is endless.

Am I embarrassed to be a pastor and have millions of people find out about my sins when they read *Heaven Is for Real*? No, I'm not embarrassed. I'm forgiven.

The other thing I've learned is that Satan is the accuser. He wants us to believe that God's patience is limited and that forgiveness comes with an expiration date. But that's not true. There's no hurt Satan can inflict that Jesus can't help. No joy he can't restore. No wrong direction he can't provide a U-turn for. Jesus, not Satan, controls the outcome.

Maybe you already know the rest of the story—how, after the resurrection, Jesus appeared on the shore while Peter and some of the other disciples were out fishing. Jesus cooked breakfast for his friends, and then he took Peter aside. Carefully and deliberately, he restored Peter from each one of his three denials. Three times he asked Peter, "Do you love me?" Three times Peter got to answer, "Yes, Lord, I do."

Then Jesus told him, "Feed my sheep." In other words, strengthen your brothers.

When we've made a mistake, he offers us the same forgiveness and restored relationship with him. And then he urges us, *strengthen the others*.

If you've never experienced Jesus' forgiveness, let me assure you, it's for real. All you have to do is ask. On the other hand, maybe you've asked for forgiveness hundreds, even thousands

*of times and have received it but now feel
reluctant to ask again. I promise you, the well
of Jesus' forgiveness is so deep it never runs out.*

*Then he said it a third time: "Simon, son of John,
do you love me?" Peter was upset that he asked
for the third time, "Do you love me?" so he
answered, "Master, you know everything there
is to know. You've got to know that I love you."
Jesus said, "Feed my sheep."*

—John 21:17–19 msg

EIGHT

Thanks for Being Imperfect

I was reminded yet again that I could be real with God, I told my fellow pastors. I learned that I didn't have to offer some kind of churchy, holy-sounding prayer in order to be heard in heaven. "You might as well tell God what you think," I said. "He already knows it anyway."

—*Heaven Is for Real*, 84

Todd

Everywhere Sonja and I go, people want to tell us about someone they've lost: a parent, a spouse . . . a child. We're very aware that while God answered our prayer and spared Colton's life, others didn't get that same answer.

We understand. After all, we lost a child too—our unborn daughter when Sonja miscarried. Why did we lose one child and not the other? I don't know. I don't think I will ever know. But I can say this: because we've been down both roads, losing a child and having a child saved, we now have two journeys to share.

I have to admit, though, that I still haven't learned enough to be any kind of expert when it comes to handling loss. I'm definitely not an experienced tour guide when it comes to grief. I struggle with it just like everyone else.

As people ask us why God answered our prayer to save Colton but he didn't save *their* child, we feel a sense of pressure, or awkwardness, or responsibility. We don't know the answer. Yet we want to give back to these people who've come to share their hearts with us. We don't want to just shrug and say, "Beats me!"

So we do what we can. Instinctively, we pray with them. Sometimes we cry with them.

As we've gone through this scene again and again, we've been amazed to have these people tell us thank you.

"Thank you?" we asked at first. It was amazing to us that, even as we continue to feel inadequate, people reassure us that we still helped them.

They thank us for having the courage to share our story despite all the critics who doubt it—and even ridicule us.

It's interesting to me that usually one of the first things these folks add after they say thank you is, "I'm glad you were honest and wrote that you questioned God. We did too. We had all those same emotions you did, and we're still trying to deal with them."

Have you ever questioned God as you've gone through a difficult time? On the other hand, has God ever done anything for you? I'm pretty sure the answer is yes. But sometimes finding the courage to share your personal story might be tough. Maybe you feel like you need to have all the answers and you don't. Maybe you feel like you're not spiritual enough or you haven't been a Christian long enough.

Maybe after you walked through your ordeal, all you can say is that God got you through it—you don't have a special message.

Let me assure you that if you're honest about your struggles and you're transparent about the events, there's someone in your life who needs to hear from you. That someone might be closer than you think—someone who may be dealing with the same problem you've been through or are going through even as you read these words. Most people we've helped have thanked us not because we're experts and not because we're great examples (we're not). They thank us for being honest about both the good and the bad.

When people are facing a trial, they find strength and support from others who have been through the same situations.

The best counselors are those who understand what you're going through, not those who have all the answers. You don't have to be an expert to help someone else. You just have to be real. Consider the simple way this formerly blind man told others what Jesus had done for him:

His neighbors and those who had formerly seen him begging asked, "Isn't this the same man who used to sit and beg?" Some claimed that he was. Others said, "No, he only looks like him." But he himself insisted, "I am the man."

"How then were your eyes opened?" they asked. He replied, "The man they call Jesus made some mud and put it on my eyes. He told me to go to Siloam and wash. So I went and washed, and then I could see."

—JOHN 9:8–11 NIV

NINE

A Mixture of Faith and Doubt

"But you were in the operating room, Colton," I said. "How could you know what we were doing?"

"'Cause I could see you," Colton said matter-of-factly. "I went up out of my body and I was looking down and I could see the doctor working on my body. And I saw you and Mommy. You were in a little room by yourself, praying; and Mommy was in a different room, and she was praying and talking on the phone."

—HEAVEN IS FOR REAL, xx–xxi

Todd

I'd like to say that when Colton first told us about his visit to heaven, I listened joyfully with a receptive mind and open heart.

But that's not what happened. I wasn't prepared for that kind of conversation with my son. Nothing in my past—no relationship, no conversation, and no class in college—had taught me how to talk with my toddler about visiting heaven.

You might think that, as a pastor, I would shout hallelujah and praise God for the glory my young son had witnessed. But let's be honest: Colton's story about seeing angels was hard to process and hard to accept, even for his pastor-daddy.

We were driving through the night to visit family several hours away when Colton told us he'd visited heaven. After some immediate surprise, the rest of the family fell asleep, and I drove through the night, thinking about what my toddler had said. To be honest, I spent most of that long night in an emotional, mental struggle.

The truth was, pastor-Daddy was struggling with faith and doubt.

As the miles passed beneath us, I tried to come up with some *other* explanation for what had happened to Colton.

Finally, as we pulled into our family's driveway in South Dakota, the word *real* was pushing its way into my head. But it was still embedded in doubt. I kept asking, *Could this be* real?

Ever been in that wrestling ring, struggling with faith and doubt? Ever wanted to believe heaven is real but then got stopped by that word *but*? Join the crowd.

But, fellow wrestler, here's the good news: God is patient with us strugglers.

Okay, so you're struggling. God understands. He knows you can't see what's waiting for you around the corner—not to mention next week or next year. But God is good at working with strugglers. Because he created us he knows where our tendency to question comes from.

The Bible tells about a dad just like me, a desperate dad who asked Jesus to heal his son. "If you can do anything, do it!" the father begged Jesus.

"*If?*" Jesus said—and I'll bet he raised his eyebrows when he said it.

The dad wanted to believe, *desperately* wanted to believe. But he was struggling. He asked Jesus to *help him believe.*

Jesus could have said, "Come back when you get your act together," or "Come back when you *know* what you believe," or, "When you get everything figured out, then come back."

But what he could have done and what he did were two different things.

All Jesus heard was that dad's simple cry: "Help me believe."

He'll hear that same prayer if it comes from you too.

> *Here is a simple prayer for you to consider praying: "Dear God, I want to believe. Please be patient with me, and help me when I struggle. Help my unbelief."*

"'If you can'?" said Jesus. "Everything is possible for one who believes."
Immediately the boy's father exclaimed, "I do believe; help me overcome my unbelief!"
> —MARK 9:23–24 NIV

TEN

Which Way You Gonna Run?

*During the quiet moments before sleep, a flood of images
tumbled through my mind—especially those horrible
moments I'd spent in that tiny room at the hospital, raging
against God. I thought I had been alone...*

—HEAVEN IS FOR REAL, 61

Todd

Yes, Colton had a glorious experience with God in
heaven. But while Colton was in heaven, where was his
pastor-daddy? Closed off in an empty hospital room, railing
against that very same God who was, at that very moment,
surrounding the pastor's son with so much love the little guy
didn't want to come back to his earthly family.

A little boy not wanting to go back to his family. Can
you imagine?

Colton's close encounter with death was the worst thing
we'd ever been through. No matter what else happened during that time, we won't ever forget that nightmare. We're

also aware that other people are living that same nightmare right now. And maybe their outcome won't be the same as ours was.

Those parents may be thinking, *Yeah, God may have saved your child, but he didn't save mine. Besides, you're a preacher, so I'm sure you've got some kind of special connection. That must be it, because God's not doing much, from my perspective.*

If you're in some closed-off place right now, railing against God, I want you to know something I learned firsthand: he's in there with you. Right there in that place, taking those verbal punches you're throwing at him. And here's something else I want you to know: he's not leaving.

When we're mad at God, that's the very time we need to be near him.

So when I went into that closed-off hospital room, furious at God because of what was happening to Colton, I had to make a decision. (We pastors get stuck in that same position you may get stuck in sometimes too. We question God.) I wanted to run, but which way was I gonna go: away from God or toward him? All I could think to do was run toward him and yell at him with everything in me, "I need you *now*."

God's ways aren't our ways. His plan isn't always plain to us. But he promises to be with us wherever we are, even in a closed-off place filled with our rage at him. He doesn't promise to take away the hard times, but if we believe in him and in his Son, and we confess our wrongdoing and accept his magnificent grace, he promises to stay with us and get us through the hard times.

Instead of saying, "God, take away the hard times," how

about saying with the psalmist, "Though I walk through the valley of the shadow of death, you are with me"?

If God doesn't seem to be with you in your hard time, ask yourself this question: Who moved?

Many of his disciples turned back and no longer followed him.
"You do not want to leave too, do you?" Jesus asked the Twelve.
Simon Peter answered him, "Lord, to whom shall we go? You have the words of eternal life."
— John 6:66–68 NIV

ELEVEN

Be Specific!

Brad Dillan called me on my cell to tell me what was going on. "What, specifically, can we pray for?" he asked.

Feeling a little odd about it, I told him what Dr. O'Holleran had said would be a good sign for Colton. So that night might be the only time in recorded history that eighty people gathered and prayed for someone to pass gas!

—*Heaven Is for Real*, 50–51

Sonja

I'm a big believer in specific prayer. I don't think I've prayed for someone to be flatulent since Colton's crisis in the hospital, but certainly our experience reinforced for me how powerful specific prayer can be, no matter how personal or intimate it is.

When it comes to talking with God, my motto is, "Ask not; have not." I don't just ask God to bless my day. I already feel like I live in a general state of blessedness all day every day. Instead, I pray for specific parts of my day, the work or activities planned, and for specific people in that day. Especially my children.

I've prayed for my kids since before they were born. The Bible says God formed them in my womb and knew them before they were born, and as I prayed for them each day of my pregnancy I got to "know" them too. I imagined their developing bodies and prayed for each part of them: their skeletons, their digestive systems, their heart and lungs, their hands and fingers. I asked God to protect them, keep them safe, and bring them safely into the world.

I'm still praying for them that way. I don't pray for something once and drop it. I'm persistent! I'm that mom who just won't stop. I like to think God recognizes my voice because it's one he hears all day every day.

And just as I prayed for my kids before they were born, I'm also praying for their marriages and their spouses long before they're married. (As I write this, Colby is only seven!)

I pray for God's protection of their future marriage, and I pray that their spouses love Jesus. I ask God to give Cassie a husband who respects and loves her and is a good leader in their home. I pray that the women Colton and Colby marry are loving and supportive.

I don't pray that they'll be in full-time ministry, although of course that would please me; but what's really important to me is that they will live their lives for Jesus and serve others. *That's* what I pray for.

And I don't just offer up specific prayers for my biological children. Every day at 3:00 p.m. I also pray for "my kids," the children in whatever Sunday school and weeknight classes I'm teaching. I set the alarm on my wristwatch, and every day when it goes off, I'm reminded to pray for those kids by name.

The thing is, many of the kids in my classes come from homes where church isn't part of their family life. They end up in my class because a friend invites them. Or a friend invites a teenager to youth group, and the younger siblings come along and end up in my class. I want to make sure that the name of each of those kids is spoken to Jesus at least once a day. I ask him to bless them, to keep them safe. And I pray that they come to know him closely and intimately.

When someone asked me recently if I pray for trivial things, like a good parking spot when I go to the mall, I had to stop and think. My conversations with God are ongoing, but I couldn't remember praying for anything like that. Still, I know that I whisper a "Thank you, Jesus!" when it's raining and a good spot opens up near the door.

Not long ago I was traveling somewhere, and as I was gathering my things to rush out the door and head for the airport, I glanced at the boarding pass I had printed from my computer. *Uh-oh*. The travel agent had misspelled my name *Sonya* instead of *Sonja*.

If you haven't flown recently, you may not know that changing an airline ticket is no easy matter, no matter what you're trying to change. Knowing all the travel warnings and restrictions that have come about since 9/11, I prayed throughout the drive to the airport that the TSA agents in the security line would realize it was just a typo and let me through. But just as I know there's power in prayer, I also know that God sometimes answers prayer in ways other than what we're asking for! So I prayed for that misspelling, and my sister-in-law Becki, our office manager and a true woman of prayer, was also praying that it would be overlooked.

And when it *was* overlooked, I whispered another fervent

"Thank you, Jesus!" prayer of gratitude as I hurried to the gate.

That's probably my most frequent specific prayer throughout the day. I want to live with an attitude of gratitude, constantly recognizing the many blessings God has given me.

> *What specific prayer do you need to*
> *start praying today for your children,*
> *your spouse, or maybe even yourself?*

You do not have because you do not ask.
—JAMES 4:2

TWELVE

The Blessing of Friends

I thought of the times where the Scripture says that God answered the prayers, not of the sick or dying, but of the friends of the sick or dying—the paralytic, for example. It was when Jesus saw the faith of the man's friends that he told the paralytic, "Get up, take your mat and go home."

—HEAVEN IS FOR REAL, 41–42

Sonja

When I'm speaking to women's groups, I talk to them about surviving the hurts that come our way. I tell them about my own crushing emotional pain when I miscarried our second child. And I describe the complete physical and emotional exhaustion I felt when Colton seemed to be dying and the doctor in North Platte told us he'd done everything he knew to do and we needed to transfer him to Omaha or Denver—just as a snowstorm rolled in, closing all the roads.

I got through those experiences only because God

granted me the strength to survive them—and because he put strong friends in my life to lift me up when I couldn't stand on my own.

I tell audiences that when something terrible happens to us, like a miscarriage or the death of an older child, we can't just curl up and die. Most of us have jobs and families. Others are depending on us, so we've got to keep going. I tell women, "We've got to get up, get through it, and get on with our lives." And we need friends every step of the way.

You can't stay in your house, closed off from everyone, after hard times hit. We weren't created to go through life alone.

Has your toddler ever told you, "I can do it myself," even when you know he or she needs help? You offer to carry that too-heavy thing the toddler wants to carry or pour that drink of juice or milk, but the toddler insists. Sometimes you give in, even though you know what's going to happen. There's gonna be a mess.

I know adults who use that same line: "I can do it myself." Sometimes it's tempting for us to believe that way. But think about this: when God created the world, he established that it is not good for man (or woman, for that matter) to be alone or to do things alone (Genesis 2:18). We need each other. Toddlers don't get it; they loudly insist, "I can do it myself!" If you're an adult and you're still living by that attitude, consider a more grown-up attitude. You *can't* do it yourself. If Jesus needed the support of his friends and disciples (and throughout the Gospels you can read where he did), then you need friends too.

I've never doubted that lesson because I lived it out as I grew up. I'm not only a pastor's wife; I'm also a pastor's kid.

My family moved every few years as Dad changed churches. So I had to learn to make friends quickly. I also learned to cherish close friends when I could find them because true, close friends don't just happen everywhere you live. You have to work at developing close friendships.

When Todd and I lived in Bartlesville, Oklahoma, I had two heart-close friends. I called Sarah my prayer partner, and I jokingly referred to Martha as my "partner in crime." We talked every day and supported each other as young wives and mothers.

Then Todd became the pastor of the church in Imperial, and we had to move. I cried all the way from Oklahoma to Nebraska, missing Martha and Sarah already and knowing I would never, ever have friends as close as they were to me.

For a while in Imperial, I struggled. As a pastor's wife, I've learned to be a little guarded about who I bring into my circle, knowing there's always the possibility that someone might want to be my friend just to have an "inside track" into the business of the church. In every town there are people who love gossip. A pastor's wife absolutely has to stay out of that kind of childish behavior, and a pastor's wife's friend has to stay out of it too.

A year went by after our move to Imperial, and although I had many acquaintances in the church and at the school where I worked, I had no close friends. I didn't feel very connected with our new hometown. In fact, at one point I went to a women's Bible study at another church, just looking for a connection. They said, "Wait, aren't you the pastor's wife at that other church across town?"

I said, "Yes, but we don't have a women's Bible study, and I need it."

I don't think they ever really accepted me as just another Christian woman wanting to soak up the Word of God. They couldn't get past my role as "the pastor's wife at that other church."

There was one woman though who, whenever I encountered her, consistently warmed my heart and made me smile. Her name was Terri, and she worked at the local bank. Like me, she had played volleyball in college, and somehow, whenever I went into the bank to cash a check or make a deposit, that connection helped us strike up conversations about all sorts of other things.

I wasn't really looking for a close friend as I chatted with Terri each week. But here's something interesting: even though I didn't feel I was actively seeking a new best friend, Todd was praying that I would find one. I didn't know that at the time. I just knew that I looked forward to going into the bank and chatting with Terri. I enjoyed talking with her about our families, about our college volleyball experiences, and gradually, about other things as well.

Terri got pregnant, and when her baby was born, I baked a loaf of banana bread and delivered it to her in the hospital. Now, for a lot of women this wouldn't be a big deal, but I am *not* one who does a lot of cooking and baking, and my oven was acting up at the time, so it was really a gift of love for me to do that. Somehow Terri understood. From that point on, our friendship grew stronger, and today, more than ten years later, she and I share a very small circle of heart-to-heart friends.

She is the perfect friend to a pastor's wife. She doesn't expect me (or my kids) to be perfect. We keep each other's kids, sometimes on a moment's notice. Colby has spent so much time at her house while Todd and I have been traveling lately that he has his own toothbrush there.

Terri is trustworthy. She doesn't ask questions about sensitive issues going on in the church, and she has a discerning heart. She probably knows far more about me, my family, and our work with the church than she would ever mention to anyone, even to me.

Oh, and best of all, she's fun! Believe me, if there's one thing a pastor's wife needs, it's occasional episodes of comic relief.

In a speaking engagement recently, I was talking about the unique and priceless gift a pastor's wife has when she has a friend she can trust, share, and laugh with. Afterward, a woman came up to me and said, "I know how hard it is to be a pastor's wife because I've been a best friend to a pastor's wife for more than twenty years."

All I could do was hug her and say thank you.

Cherish your friends. You're going to need them when you're climbing out of the pit. And if you don't have a close friend right now, I encourage you to work on finding one.

*If you need a friend, start praying, and watch
for God to bring someone into your life who can
be that friend you need. Then you be the friend
she needs as well. Don't have a toddler's I-can-
do-it-myself mind-set. Remember that even
Jesus needed the help and support of others.*

*[Jesus] took Peter and the two sons of Zebedee
with him, and he began to be very sad and*

troubled. He said to them, "My heart is full of sorrow, to the point of death. Stay here and watch with me."

—Matthew 26:37–38 ncv

THIRTEEN

Give Anyway

With $23,000 in bills due and payable immediately, we didn't know what we were going to do. Sonja and I discussed asking our bank for a loan, but it turned out we didn't need to.

—HEAVEN IS FOR REAL, 55

Todd

Don't you just love generous people who are cheerful givers? Sonja and I were those people before our lives got turned upside down by medical crises. We didn't have a lot of money, but we had a strong habit of giving what we could. Giving to our church and to the charities and individuals we supported came first each month when we sat down to pay the monthly bills. We considered it giving to God—or rather, giving *back* to God, because we believe everything we have is a gift from him.

But after my own medical expenses for a broken leg, kidney stones, and a cancer scare, all requiring time off from work, and then Colton's two surgeries, things looked different when we faced those bills. We didn't have enough money to pay the thirty-two-hundred-dollar deductible on Colton's biggest medical bill, let alone the more than twenty thousand dollars in other payments due that month.

So the question that day was, were we going to give back to God that month or hold on to what little we had for ourselves?

Despite the numbers we were looking at, it wasn't a hard decision. We gave anyway.

After all, God had just given us back our son. We didn't have a lot of money, but we had Colton. There was no way we were going to stop giving to a God who had done that for us. If we were headed for bankruptcy, okay. But we had our son.

You can always find a reason to give to God when you realize what he's done for you. On the other hand, I guess you can always find a reason *not* to give to God if that's what you're looking for. I could have looked at what I *didn't* have—twenty-three thousand dollars. Instead, I looked at what I *did* have: my son.

Here's the truth: God responds to giving, no matter how small the gift or how bad your circumstances. I believe God blesses givers. And he loves it when we can be *cheerful* givers.

Most people in bad situations think, *If I could win the lottery, then I'll give.* The truth is, whether you have little or much, giving should be the same decision, the same habit. Even when you think you can't, give anyway.

What if our outcome had been different? What if I didn't have my son? Did I still have reasons to give? Yes, two big reasons: First, I looked at who was holding my son on his lap when I thought I was losing him. Second, I looked at who gave his Son for me.

So even if I didn't have my son, would I still have had a reason to give?

What do *you* think?

If you're in a hard place today, don't give up on giving. Give anyway.

This most generous God who gives seed to the farmer that becomes bread for your meals is more than extravagant with you. He gives you something you can then give away.
        —2 CORINTHIANS 9:9–10 MSG

FOURTEEN

A Journey through Humility

Our "tenth" bills are one of the cool things about living in a small town. On the other hand, when you can't pay, it's a lot more humbling.

—*Heaven Is for Real*, 54

Todd

We didn't come close to having the money we owed after Colton's (and my own) medical crises. We owed not only hospital, doctor, and other medical bills but also our normal monthly expenses, many of which were owed to businesses in our hometown.

In a place like Imperial, Nebraska, population 2,071, businesses like the gas station, the grocery store, and the hardware store let trusted customers charge purchases and services to a personal account. My family is honored to be part of that "trusted" group. On the tenth of the month, one of us, usually Sonja, drives around town to settle the accounts and pay what we owe. But the month after Colton's emergency surgery and hospital stay, there wasn't enough money to go around.

We could have just let things slide, assuming that the businesses we patronized were aware of our situation and could stand to wait a month or two to be paid. But of course, that wasn't the right way to handle things. We needed to talk with each merchant face-to-face. And I couldn't put that job on Sonja. Yes, we both work, but as the husband and dad, I feel the ultimate responsibility to support my family. And believe me, going around town to apologize for failing at that duty and then asking for an extension was humbling but necessary.

Yes, most people knew the challenges we had been through. Most of them were not just our merchants; they were also our friends. If we hadn't paid those bills, they would probably have carried us over to the next month without penalty, maybe without even saying anything or mailing us a bill. But I didn't want to betray the trust they had put in us.

We did have some things going for us. Most important was our record. This was our first time to default. That kind of record made it a lot easier to go around and ask for help—ask for mercy, really, saying, "I'm sorry. I know I owe you this money, but we've just been through a really hard time, and I'm not able to pay this bill. But you can trust that I *will* pay you as soon as I can."

I had to admit my need for mercy, and it's never easy to do that.

Some of us have that same dread when we need to ask God for mercy after we've let him down in some way. It may be the last thing we want to do, to come before our powerful God and say, "I messed up, Lord."

But we need to remember that he already knows we've fallen short of what he expected of us or that we've made a mistake in some way. He also knows our situation surrounding that mistake or shortcoming as well, just like our hometown creditors knew the Burpos' circumstances. But *confession* is an essential part of apologizing and asking for mercy, both in our everyday activities here on earth and in our spiritual lives too.

Admitting your need for mercy, when you have a legitimate reason to ask for it, can be a cleansing act. It can move others to help you when they might not be so inclined if you hadn't taken that first step into humility. Even bill collectors, if you call them first instead of waiting until they call you, are sometimes amazingly understanding. Sometimes they will even reduce what is owed.

Here's a difference we need to recognize between earth and heaven: humility *might* move someone down here to help you, but it will *always* move the God who sits on the throne of heaven to help you. The Bible says God wants to pour out his grace on us, but there's this big obstacle: our pride. If we get past our pride, get on our knees, and say, "God, I need you," he always responds. Not sometimes, but always. God *always* responds to that kind of humility.

Look at these words from the apostle John. He's talking about humility, confession, and forgiveness. And he nails it. It's not that God might forgive you. It's that he will forgive you.

*If we confess our sins, he will forgive our sins,
because we can trust God to do what is right. He
will cleanse us from all the wrongs we have done.*

—1 JOHN 1:9 NCV

FIFTEEN

No Secrets

*"I was sitting by God the Holy Spirit because I was praying
for you. You needed the Holy Spirit, so I prayed for you."*
—HEAVEN IS FOR REAL, 102

Todd

I closed the door of the empty hospital room so no one
could hear or see me except the target of my rage: God. And
there, in the privacy of that room, I let him have it, raging
and railing at him for seeming to dump my son at death's
door.

In that private, hidden place, I behaved in a way I would
not have wanted anyone else to hear—certainly not the
members of the church I pastored or anyone in my family.
Especially not my children.

And yet Colton *did* see. He told us later that while he
was on the operating table, "I went up out of my body and
I was looking down. . . . I saw you and Mommy. You were
in a little room by yourself, praying. . . ."

Colton's words shocked me. It's one thing to think that God can see and hear everything I do and say. We expect that. But to think that our loved ones in heaven also may be able to see and hear some or all of what we say and do—*that* really bothers me.

Here's one reason why. Sometime later Colton and my mom and I were sitting at the table, and Mom asked Colton if Jesus had said anything about his dad being a pastor. Colton said yes, he did. Then he started telling her about an experience I had when I was thirteen.

Thirteen!

Now you tell me, would you want *your* mom to know all the stuff you did when *you* were thirteen? For me, at least, that could be pretty embarrassing! I was sitting there, dumbfounded, until I had the presence of mind to yell, "*Stopppp!* Okay, we need to leave the room and take a break."

Believe me, no matter how old you get, there are just some things you don't want your mom to find out.

I didn't want that little sharing session to turn into a tattling session. Well, Colton wasn't tattling, of course. He was just telling, matter-of-factly, what Jesus had told him. But for me it was a rather awkward moment—and also an enlightening one, because I realized Colton had been allowed to see my past. Later we would learn he also saw a part of my future.

The knowledge that my loved ones in heaven may be part of what the Bible calls "so great a cloud of witnesses"— our family and friends, along with God—who see and know everything about me is, well, it's pretty humbling. And also motivating—another reason to be mindful of my words and actions.

Jesus wants us to win, to cross the line, victorious, and join him in heaven. Our loved ones in heaven want the same thing for us. They're not watching like Big Brother, hoping to catch us making a mistake.

As a student, I had teachers who seemed to want their students to fail. They'd brag about how difficult their exams were and say things like, "You're gonna blow this." Other teachers, however, wanted their students to succeed, even when the test *was* difficult. That's the attitude of the "so great a cloud of witnesses" watching us from heaven. They're rooting for us, praying for us. They want us to win, and they're cheering for us, just like we cheer when we watch our kids run a race or compete in some sport.

When I thought I was all alone in that hospital room, struggling through the most difficult time in my life, Colton, sitting in heaven beside the Holy Spirit, saw me. "You needed the Holy Spirit, so I prayed for you," he told me later. Think how unnatural that was for a child his age to say and do. But that's exactly what Colton said and did. It's what your loved ones are doing for you too. The next time you're in the midst of a hard time, remember that.

How many family members do you have in heaven who are praying for you— parents, grandparents, siblings? Picture them cheering for you as you confront difficulties here on earth. Know that they are praying for you to cross that finish line, victorious, and join them there.

Therefore we also, since we are surrounded by so great a cloud of witnesses, let us lay aside every weight, and the sin which so easily ensnares us, and let us run with endurance the race that is set before us.

—HEBREWS 12:1

SIXTEEN

Find Your Own Faith

Pastor Butcher was a short, bald, lively preacher—energetic and engaging, not dull and dry the way kids sometimes expect an older pastor to be. He challenged the group of 150 teenagers that night: "There are some of you here tonight whom God could use as pastors and missionaries."

The memory of that moment of my life is one of those crystal-clear ones, distilled and distinct, like the moment you graduate from high school or your first child is born. I remember that the crowd of kids faded away and the reverend's voice receded into the background. I felt a pressure in my heart, almost a whisper: That's you, Todd. That's what I want you to do.

—HEAVEN IS FOR REAL, 91

Todd

I was thirteen and attending church camp in Arkansas when, all of a sudden during the pastor's message, God himself spoke to my heart. Even though I was surrounded by other teenagers, I was hearing God's voice speak directly to me. I was still in the room with everyone else, but part of me wasn't there anymore.

Such moments are hard to explain to others who haven't experienced them. At thirteen, my heart raced and my palms sweated as I sensed God saying something like, "Yeah, Todd, I'm talking to *you*."

I was raised in a Christian family and had grown up (at least as grown up as you can be at thirteen) accepting my parents' beliefs. But to *accept* something and to *understand* something are two different things. For me, God became real when I felt he was speaking directly to me.

You may have read or heard others describe their life-changing moments with God. Truly, hearing God speak to us on an individual basis is powerful. It reminds us how much we matter to God.

As I have grown older, these God moments seem much more natural and far less dramatic. But they are still the highlight of my walk with Christ.

That moment I had with God when I was thirteen was very dramatic. But it wasn't my first. My first one-on-one conversation with God that I can remember occurred when I was nine. I was at a different camp, and it was hot, humid, and fun. In a service there, God took over the speaker's voice. Honestly. That's how it was for me. My pulse raced and my hands shook—I vividly remember that—but I overcame my jitters and responded to the invitation to accept Jesus into my heart. And at that moment, I knew without a doubt that God was real, and my faith was my own.

It wasn't something I did just because I knew it would please my parents. I wanted to follow God *for myself*.

Colton "found" his own faith during his visit to heaven. Obviously, during that experience God proved to Colton that he was real. Today there's no way you could talk Colton out of his belief in God or his trip to heaven. He knows that he knows, and nothing will ever change that.

I don't know exactly how you pass God on to others so that they find their own personal faith. You can't just hand faith over like you can give someone a slice of pizza or a cold soda. Only the readiness of a person's heart and the presence of God himself can cause someone to believe for himself or herself.

As a parent, I had two responses to Colton's personal awareness of God. First, I was thrilled that he had made his own personal contact with God. Second, I was a little bit jealous. He had made that contact when he was only three, and obviously, Colton's contact was way deeper than my first direct connection with God had been. But my gratefulness for Colton's personal faith far outweighed any real envy I might have had.

And then there was the day when our youngest child, Colby, came to my bedroom doorway with a dead-serious look on his face. He was only five, but it was obvious he had something really important to share.

"Dad, can I ask you a question?" he asked.

I had barely finished my shower; I had a towel wrapped around me and water still dripping down my face. But seeing Colby's seriousness, I nodded and waited for what he had to say.

With big brown eyes looking up at me, Colby said, "I've just been talking to God. Can you pray with me, Dad? I want to be a Christian too."

Talk about *Wow*! I might not have been suitably dressed

for that life-changing event, but I will never forget that moment. I'm not sure what God had said to Colby, but once again I was thrilled. God-contact had been made!

Still wearing nothing but a towel, I called Sonja to the room, and we both prayed with Colby that morning.

I've noticed that children seem to be ready to "get" God faster than adults. As we age, we become more cynical, more closed, and more self-reliant. As time passes, the world seems to bruise us and cause our once-soft hearts to harden.

Whenever I have a conversation with people who doubt God's existence, I suggest that they pray (if they pray at all), asking God to prove himself. I tell them, "Just pray, 'God, if you're real, prove it to me. And show me that Jesus is your Son.'"

Now, I know some people are simply not honest enough to pray that prayer and really mean it. I guess you have to be the judge about your own honesty level. But look at it this way: you have nothing to lose by praying that prayer!

Still, I want to warn you—I really want you to know—that if you're honest and you truly desire an answer, God *is* going to answer.

It might take some time for God to answer your prayer. And I certainly won't predict how he might. But I will tell you that I'm praying with you even now: "God, please speak to the willing heart who is honestly praying this prayer!" If you have doubts about God, ask him to prove himself to you. You have everything to gain, and nothing to lose.

You will seek me and find me when you seek me with all your heart.

—JEREMIAH 29:13 NIV

SEVENTEEN

Lead-Footed Preacher's Wife

Sonja was serving as a pastor's wife, a full-time job in itself, plus as a mom, teacher, library volunteer, and secretary for the family business.

—HEAVEN IS FOR REAL, 117

Sonja

Todd often describes how, when he was thirteen years old, he felt God telling him he wanted Todd to be a pastor when he grew up. I don't remember having a specific moment during my youth when I realized what I would be when I grew up. All I can tell you is that I grew up knowing I would be a pastor's wife.

My dad is a pastor and my brother is a pastor, so being a pastor's wife seemed like a perfectly natural role for me. But, as any pastor's wife can tell you, it's not an easy role to fill.

There used to be a joke—well, maybe it wasn't a joke, and maybe in some places it's still a requirement—that the main qualification for being a pastor's wife was that you had to know how to play the piano. Yes, I play. And yes, I've played for church many, many times (including several times when I was as sick as a dog but showed up anyway). Thankfully, I've retired from that duty now, but I always want to be supportive of Todd in whatever way he needs me.

Playing the piano for church services isn't nearly the biggest challenge pastors' wives face. That talent actually falls pretty far down the list, below a couple of bigger "qualifications," including the ability to live and raise your family in the spotlight and having a heart big enough to share your family with the congregation.

It's a no-brainer that pastors and their wives and children are held to a higher standard of behavior than non-churched families may be. The Christian faith is all about striving to model Christ in all areas of your life—showing humility in all things, having a servant's heart, and, well, to put it bluntly, not breaking any laws or making headlines due to scandalous behavior!

The fact is, people in the church can blow it and be forgiven, but if a pastor—or sometimes a pastor's family member—blows it, that pastor most likely will be fired. It's not right for the church to have that attitude, but Jesus is the "gold standard" for pastors, and too often pastors and their families are expected to meet that standard.

Well, I'm sorry, but only Jesus was without sin. Certainly pastors should be good examples, and ideally their families too. But all believers are supposed to be good examples, not just pastors and their families, and it just isn't right for that double standard to be imposed on them. I don't know of any other families, except maybe politicians', that get exposed for their mistakes the way pastors and their families do. It's really hard.

If you're breathing, you're human (and that includes pastors and their families), and you make mistakes. I know one pastor's wife who makes a lot of them—me. And the mistake I make most often is *speeding*.

Yes, I have a lead foot. I'm always in a hurry, and to be honest, I've seen those red lights flashing in my rearview mirror many more times than a preacher's wife (or anyone else) should. I've been stopped in Nebraska, South Dakota, Oklahoma, Kansas, Colorado, and Texas. There might be another one I forgot.

People who know me know that this is one of my failings and, thank God, they don't condemn me for it—at least not too much.

Not long ago we had to catch a flight out of Denver, normally a three-hour drive from Imperial. Todd was telling someone that we got a late start and made it in two hours and forty minutes.

"Oh, was Sonja driving?" the friend asked. (Actually I wasn't driving that time, but it goes to show my reputation around here.)

On a different trip not too long ago I got another ticket. The officer who pulled me over asked, "Do you know how fast you were going?"

"Nope," I answered innocently.

"Seventy-two," he said. Then he mentioned something about it being a 60 mph zone.

"Why were you in such a hurry?" he asked.

"I want to get home," I told him.

Mercifully, he reduced the ticket to a different category so the fine didn't cost as much. Todd and both boys were in the car with me when it happened, and amazingly, neither

Colton nor Colby remembered to tell Cassie about it. But she didn't stay in the dark for long. This week, while I was out of town, I got a text message from her that said, "Did you get a speeding ticket last week!"

Apparently a couple of her friends had seen my name in the local newspaper. Who knew teenagers read the newspaper?

Besides my tendency to speed, the other big challenge I struggle with as a pastor's wife is being gracious about sharing my husband. Even though I grew up seeing the demands on a pastor's time and watched how well my mom modeled patience and acceptance, I really had no idea how hard that requirement would be. The fact is, a pastor is always on call. There's probably not a pastor alive who hasn't had a meal or a vacation or a night's sleep interrupted by a phone call from a church member (and sometimes even non–church members) who need his or her help.

Pastors sometimes miss their kids' school programs or sporting events because they're preaching funerals. They miss meals because they're at the bedside of someone who is dying. They miss their children's dance recitals and baseball games because they're comforting other kids' parents about some crisis that has happened. It's just the way things are. I get that. It's been a struggle sometimes, but over the years I've become resolved to it. I still can't say I like it, but when Todd and I were married in 1990 and I was asked, "Do you take this man . . . ?" I understood that I was also "taking" his church.

And speaking of *taking*, a pastor's wife also has to learn to "take it" when her husband is criticized unfairly or accused of favoritism or targeted with other complaints.

I'm not saying I don't defend Todd in some of those circumstances, but I do have to be very careful how I respond.

The truth is, I never, ever want to keep someone from coming to Jesus or being impacted by Jesus because I'm having a hissy fit about some unfair criticism or throwing myself a pity party insisting that he stay home instead of doing his job.

As I said, I've resolved myself to sharing Todd with our church. That's a given. But since the release of *Heaven Is for Real* there's been a huge new demand on his time, and I have to admit, I'm struggling to cope with it. We both believe that Colton's visit to heaven is a story that God expects us to share. So we wrote the book, and to date, nearly seven million copies of the original book and more than five hundred thousand copies of the children's version have been sold. People read the book and want to know more; churches and other groups invite Todd to come and talk about Colton's experience and how it has impacted our lives and millions of others'.

So now I'm not just sharing him with our local congregation. I'm sharing him with the world. And that's hard. *Really* hard. It's hard because Todd's not here with the kids and me, and we need him and miss him. But it's also hard because, even though he travels surrounded by the prayers of our church, our family, and our friends, as his wife I can't help but worry about him amid the ordinary dangers of travel.

I'm writing this in late winter, during a week when Todd is on the road. He was on a flight coming into Milwaukee on a foggy morning when the plane missed its approach and had to pull up and go around and make a second attempt. The plane did land safely, but the danger was not over. The day was so foggy that the airport had trucks parked along the runway and taxiway to shine their headlights to guide the plane into the gates. Hearing Todd describe it later, I thanked God for his mercy—and for guiding those skilled pilots, flight controllers, and ground crews who brought Todd's flight in safely.

But dangerous travel conditions aren't my only worries when Todd is away. We know there are people who don't believe Colton's story and don't like that we've told it to the world in what we see as our responsibility to share the love of Jesus. We know they don't like it because they've contacted us and told us so—and even threatened us. So again, as a wife and mother, I worry.

Invitations have come in for me to speak publicly as well—sharing Colton's story and how it has impacted our family and so many others. I am not a public speaker. I've never wanted to be and still don't feel comfortable doing it. Accepting those invitations pulls me way out of my safety zone. Yet I feel God telling me that's what he wants me to do—join Todd in spreading the message of hope that comes from the experience God gave our family.

So I've also been out on the road for a few appearances. I try to schedule these engagements during times our kids don't have some kind of school or sports competition, but that's hard to do with three kids involved in a wide range of activities. I joked to one audience recently that I had missed Cassie's district softball tournament the year before because I was away from home, speaking somewhere, and that "I'm still in therapy because of it."

I decline more invitations than I accept, believing that my first responsibility is to support Todd in the work he's doing both in our local church and in his travels around the country. But it's also important to me to be a mother to our three children. I also work as office manager in a local real estate firm. So yes, I'm busy.

If you're in a church with a hardworking pastor, you're probably also in a church with a hardworking pastor's wife. I hope you'll do your part to support her (or him) with your love and encouragement—and with mercy and grace if you happen to see that person's name in the newspaper's traffic court list.

Consider doing something nice for your pastor's family today. I've been blown away by the kindness of our congregation, whether it's a bouquet of flowers sent just to me or members showing up to clean our house. These are gifts this lead-footed pastor's wife always appreciates!

Give a bonus to leaders who do a good job, especially the ones who work hard at preaching and teaching.

—1 TIMOTHY 5:17 MSG

EIGHTEEN

Prayers for the Hopeless

[The nurse] seemed to hesitate for a moment; then she plunged on. "But seeing your boy the way he is today, this is a miracle. There has to be a God, because this is a miracle."

—*HEAVEN IS FOR REAL, 148*

Todd

The words of two women came a few hours apart and were a contrast in extremes. Sonja's words came first: "I can't do this anymore!" she said that night when Colton's doctor told us there was nothing else they could do—right as that snowstorm rolled in, keeping us from transferring him to a bigger hospital.

Just then a friend called to tell us that church members were gathered back in our hometown to pray for Colton. Within sixty minutes, those prayers were answered.

By morning, we had cycled from frantically desperate to completely normal, and Colton was up, smiling and chipper, happily playing with his action figures.

The doctor was astonished, and so were the nurses. One of them, a hospital veteran, pulled me aside and said, "I'm not supposed to tell you this, but we were told not to give your family any encouragement. They didn't think Colton was going to make it. And when they tell us people aren't going to make it, they don't."

That's when she said Colton's recovery was a miracle and that it convinced her "there has to be a God."

She didn't have all the details worked out in her mind yet, but she was ready to consider that there might be a God. She had the evidence she needed to start the work toward believing.

I was shocked to hear that the nurses had been told not to give us any hope for Colton's recovery. Of course *we* still had hope—because we still had prayer, our own and dozens of others.

Those prayers in a hopeless situation were answered. And not only was the hopeless situation resolved, but it might be that the life of someone watching was changed for the better as well.

What do you suppose is going on in the world right now that might seem hopeless, except to those who are pounding on heaven's doors with their prayers? Let me put it to you in another, more personal way: what do you *know* is going on in *your* world right now that seems hopeless?

Maybe you're not the type who's able to openly share struggles or pain, or maybe you don't have people close enough to you who have offered to pray with you when hard times hit. There are far too many people in this world who don't have anyone to pray with them and for them.

May *I* pray for you? Go to HIFRMinistries.org and

click on "Prayer Request." My prayer team and I would be glad to knock on heaven's doors for you.

Who are you praying for?
Who's praying for you?

Where two or three are gathered together in My name, I am there in the midst of them.
—MATTHEW 18:20

NINETEEN

Life as a Sermon

She didn't need [to hear] a sermon—she'd already seen one.
—HEAVEN IS FOR REAL, 148

Todd and Sonja

There's something else we want to point out about that incident where the nurse told me Colton's recovery was a miracle and "there has to be a God." It's linked to the two messages we share when we're speaking to audiences around the country. During those appearances, Sonja reminds listeners that everyone has a story, a testimony about what God has done for him or her. Your story may not come in a book with a yellow cover and a cute little boy on the front, but that doesn't mean it's not as real as our story is. We all have stories of what God has done in our lives, and by sharing that story we can inspire and encourage others who may be stuck in a crisis or heartbreaking part of their story.

Combine that truth with what Todd tells audiences: he

says that too often in the church we have a messed-up perception that pastors and missionaries are the only ones with a *calling* to share the gospel.

Yes, God's call to pastors and missionaries is unique, but whether you're a plumber or electrician, hotel maid or restaurant dishwasher, schoolteacher or stay-at-home parent, building janitor or corporate executive, you have a calling too. There is not one person who doesn't have a calling to impact others with God's message of love, grace, and the promise of heaven.

Maybe your calling is to influence and encourage coworkers. Maybe it's an after-work calling, like Sonja's, to the children in your church. Maybe it's to the folks living in nursing homes or assisted living facilities. Or maybe you're homebound and your calling is to pray for those in need. Discover your own calling through prayer and by considering what you enjoy doing and who you enjoy being with. Then watch for God to open up opportunities for you.

I (Todd) have shared my story of how I felt God calling me to be a pastor—and I enjoy preaching. But for most folks, having a calling has nothing to do with preaching. And even God's call to preachers isn't solely about preaching. Instead, a calling means God asks us to live so that we touch others' lives for him.

That's how the most powerful sermons are shared. The nurse in the hospital who told me, "There has to be a God because this is a miracle" probably wouldn't have had the same reaction if I had simply met her out on the street somewhere and *told* her what happened—that friends back home were joining us in praying for Colton and that what happened next was nothing short of miraculous. Instead, she saw that "sermon" quietly played out, and as a result, she became convinced that God is real.

The nurse saw us praying, and she saw our church friends coming in and out of the hospital. I've been told that in that hospital they can tell when a patient comes in from our congregation because they see the same praying, supportive people there visiting and encouraging the patient and his or her family.

In fact, our church custodian had surgery there, and recently she told me later that when the doctor came in to check on her that night, maybe after seeing familiar church family and friends there earlier, he smiled and said, "You go to Todd's church, don't you?"

Those people who keep showing up at that hospital to pray for and support each other are making an impact on the hospital staff, who are seeing a sermon lived out.

Sonja

Miracles are great. And so is living your life as a sermon. But we don't want you to think you can never make a mistake or that you have to have a college degree or be a Bible scholar to make your life, or your story, a testimony. Look at Colton. Here's a kid who tells his story very simply. He doesn't elaborate. He doesn't go into deep explanations. He just says, matter-of-factly, this is what happened. (If the old police show *Dragnet* were still on the air, he could definitely be a stand-in for that detective who would say, "Just the facts, ma'am.")

Colton's story, which he tells with unadorned, childlike innocence, has convinced thousands of people that heaven is for real. It shows that people don't need to see a miracle.

They can just hear the unshakable faith of a child and know he's telling the truth. And that's enough.

There are many ways to reach someone for God. What many adults need to realize is that God doesn't need us to *argue* for him. He doesn't expect us to have all the answers. He just wants us to share our story, in the simplest terms possible, and to tell people what he has done for us, and then show them by how we live that he's at work in our lives. He'll take care of the rest.

Todd

I was on a cross-country flight recently and the woman I sat next to spotted the yellow *Heaven Is for Real* bracelet I wear. She looked at me, recognized my face from pictures she'd seen, and said, "You wrote the book, didn't you?"

I smiled and said, "Did you like it?"

She said, "Well, I just came back from Palestine. I have extended family there. I used that book with my family. It was the first time I can remember that we sat down and talked about God without getting into a fight."

Who knows how—or whom—your story, or your life, will impact? You might be leading someone to heaven. There's always room there for more!

*Watch for openings when someone might
be receptive to believing merely by hearing
your simply told story of how God has
recently touched your own life.*

I, too, give witness to the greatness of God, our
Lord, high above all other gods. He does just as he
pleases—however, wherever, whenever.

—PSALM 135:5–6 MSG

TWENTY

It's the People

When I peeked into Harold's room, I saw Daniel and Gloria, along with three or four family members, including a couple I knew to be Harold's other daughters....

I turned to Harold's bed and saw that he was lying very still, drawing in deep breaths, spaced at wide intervals. I had seen men and women at this phase of the end of life many times. When they reach their last moments, they slip in and out of consciousness and even while awake, in and out of lucidity.

I turned to Gloria. "How's your dad doing?" I asked.

"He's hanging on, but I don't think he has much longer," she said.

—HEAVEN IS FOR REAL, 118

Todd

After surviving something serious, the smaller, everyday stuff that used to be upsetting or annoying just doesn't get as much of your time or attention as it once did. At least that's how it has worked for Sonja and me. And there's another thing too: your sense of value changes.

I know people whose main goal in life is to have a great car or a big house or the newest red or green tractor. (Yeah, I live in Nebraska.) But I'm guessing a lot of those people haven't stood by a hospital bedside, screaming at God not to take their child.

After that kind of experience, you tend to forget about the little things—and you realize life isn't about *things* anyway. To correct a well-known political insider's slogan from a few presidential campaigns ago, "It's the people, stupid!"

Wise people learn this lesson and live this truth before they reach the end of their life. When you "get" what's important, you start investing more of yourself in the people in your life: the ones you love and the ones who love you back.

Life is short. Sometimes *too* short.

But however old you are when you get to the end of your life, maybe you'll be like my friend Harold, described in the excerpt above, who was lying in a nursing home bed, suspended between this life and the next. At that point, you won't be asking for the plaques you earned, the trophies you won, the stuff you collected. What's going to matter then is the people you love. That's what you'll want around you as you head off into eternity.

If you don't know it now, you'll know it then: it's the people in your life who matter.

*Who do you need to find and give
a hug to today or maybe send a
"thinking of you" note or e-mail?*

*A new command I give you: Love one another. As
I have loved you, so you must love one another.*
— JOHN 13:34 NIV

TWENTY-ONE

At Home in Heaven

I laid my hand on the old minister's shoulder, closed my eyes, and prayed aloud, reminding God of Harold's long and faithful service, asking that the angels would make his journey quick and smooth, and that God would receive his servant with great joy. When I finished the prayer, I turned to rejoin the family. . . .

Colton peered earnestly up into Harold's face and said, "It's going to be okay. The first person you're going to see is Jesus."

—*HEAVEN IS FOR REAL*, 119

Todd

Have you ever flown somewhere, maybe at holiday time, when the airport's arrival area is jam-packed with happily expectant friends and family members—but no one's there to meet your flight? I've done a lot of traveling since *Heaven Is for Real* was published, and I can tell you, there's a big difference in coming into a bustling airport where you don't know anyone—and arriving at an airport where someone comes striding up with a smiling face, eagerly greeting you and welcoming you to that place.

Heaven is also a big, busy place—bigger than anyplace we've ever seen. Isn't it reassuring to know that Jesus will come and take you there when it's your time to go? You won't have to look around, trying to find him or trying to find your way to heaven. Picture him right there, extending his hand and welcoming you. You don't have to program your spiritual GPS or anything!

Equally comforting is the fact that Jesus will also be there to welcome our loved ones into glory: elderly grandparents whose earthly dementia kept them from finding their way from one room to the next, innocent children who'd never gone anywhere alone before, beloved family members who may have been snatched from this world to the next by accident or violence. Jesus will be there, his face aglow, his confidence contagious, telling our friends and family members what Colton told our dear friend Harold Greer: "It's going to be okay. The first person you're going to see is Jesus."

The moment we arrive in heaven, all our fear, all our worries will be removed. And from that moment on, throughout eternity, it's going to be okay.

I joke with Colton that whenever a woman comes up to him somewhere to talk about his story, he knows he's gonna get the dreaded "feeling" question: "Colton, what did heaven *feel* like?"

It's a joke for us guys because, you know, talking about our feelings isn't something we're real comfortable with. (And if you think it's hard to get a grown man to talk about his feelings, just try getting an adolescent boy to open up!)

But Colton expects the question now, and his answer comes honestly and easily. He tells the simple truth: "When I was in heaven, it felt like I was home."

When you leave this earth, are you leaving home or going home?

I will come back and take you to be with me that you also may be where I am.

—JOHN 14:3 NIV

TWENTY-TWO

Heaven—You're Gonna Like It

His tone was matter-of-fact, as though he were describing something as real and familiar as the town fire station. Daniel and Gloria exchanged looks and a surreal feeling washed over me. By then I was used to hearing Colton talk about heaven. But now he had become a messenger, a tiny tour guide for a departing heavenly traveler.

—Heaven Is for Real, 119

Todd

We all want to go to heaven. Someday. Just not today. At least that's what many popular songs say today on the radio airwaves. Sometimes I listen to country music, and I've noticed there's a popular song Kenny Chesney sings, "Everybody Wants to Go to Heaven But Nobody Wants to Go Now." I don't care what genre you listen to, though, you've probably heard a song that carries the same message.

Colton is the exception to this general idea of wanting to go to heaven *someday*. One of the most amazing

things about him is the steady, unshakable hope he carries with him. This is one kid who would like to go back
to heaven *now*.

I don't know about you, but I grew up thinking, *Yeah,
heaven's a good place, and I want to go there*. But to be
honest, I couldn't get too excited about the traditional
view that we'd live in mansions and walk on streets paved
with gold. Probably like a lot of people, I wondered, *Will
we play harps and float on clouds all day, or what?* I
knew that being with Jesus throughout eternity would be
a wonderful thing, but frankly, I just couldn't grasp *how*
wonderful it could be. It just seemed too huge an idea to
understand.

Then my son came back from heaven with such strong
eagerness to go back that he lost all fear of death.

What does that tell you?

If a little kid feels that way, you just know heaven has
to be *fun*. And if it's that appealing to a kid, what will it be
like for adults? For everyone?

I think it means heaven will be custom-made for *me*.
And for *you*. It won't be a place where we sit around all
day and sing "Kumbaya" (unless maybe you *like* the idea of
sitting around all day and singing it). It'll be a place that's
interesting, engaging, and amazing. It's hard to think of
words to describe how it's surely going to feel.

Most of all, I think, in heaven we'll feel *secure*. Forever.
We'll be with Jesus, the all-powerful King, and we won't have
to lock the doors or set a security alarm. We won't have to
worry about getting cancer or diabetes. We won't ever be
betrayed by a loved one, attacked by an assailant, or run over
by a car. We'll be safe from all harm.

We'll also be productive. Since Colton was given homework while he was in heaven, he assures me all of us will be assigned a job to do, something we enjoy. Our work there will reward us with sense of purpose, productivity, and accomplishment.

Most of all, in heaven we'll feel *loved*. Colton tells me, "Dad, in heaven, you can just feel God's love all the time."

As a pastor, I've seen a lot of people who've shown an eagerness for heaven. But almost all of them were suffering and longed for death to bring relief from their misery and pain. Maybe it was cancer. Maybe loneliness. Maybe old age or dementia. All these sufferers wanted something better, and they looked forward to heaven as a place where their suffering or sadness would end.

What I saw in Colton when he was four, and what I'm still seeing in him now that he's a teenager, is a completely different kind of anticipation. His life right now, for the most part, is pretty good. But he still longs for heaven.

Fortunately, dads can learn from their kids. Absorbing all the information about heaven I've learned from Colton, I now long for heaven more eagerly too. What about you?

Another song that's good to listen to when troubles weigh you down is Carrie Underwood's "This Is My Temporary Home."

I want to leave this life and be with Christ, which is much better, but you need me here in my body.
—Philippians 1:23–24 ncv

TWENTY-THREE

Heavenly Comforters

Then he grew serious. "Dad, Jesus had the angels sing to me because I was so scared. They made me feel better."

—*HEAVEN IS FOR REAL, XIX*

Sonja

Colton wasn't the first person to be comforted by angels in a scary place. The Bible tells us on the first Christmas night, shepherds staying out in their fields with their sheep were terrified by the "glory of the Lord" that suddenly surrounded them. I imagine a little boy would probably be just as scared when he found himself in a strange place.

The angels sang to Colton when he was in the hospital operating room, anesthetized, and about to be taken up to heaven. A lot of people who have a near-death experience talk about a white light or a long tunnel and a sense of peace. But here's a little kid saying, "I was so scared."

He was scared of the unknown, scared of what was happening to him. Most noticeable to me in all this is that Colton was totally honest about what he was feeling. His experience makes me think about what happens when we adults admit that we're scared about something. What happens when we're totally honest with ourselves and with God?

The Bible says God is looking for worshippers who worship him "in spirit and *truth*" (John 4:24; italics mine). When we come before God with truthful spirits, that's the point where he can deal with our honest feelings. Of course he already knows what's going on inside us, but he addresses those feelings when we honestly bring them before him.

So picture Colton suddenly finding himself in heaven. Since he's a little boy, he doesn't know any better than to express his honest feelings: *I'm scared.*

Then what's the first thing Jesus did for him? He addressed that need. He sent his angels to sing to Colton.

The lesson for us is that Jesus will comfort us too when we're scared, even before we get to heaven. Whether we're scared about our child's health or our own, our job or our finances—whatever is scaring you, bring it to Jesus in honest prayer and trust that he will respond to your need in exactly the way that works best for you.

> *God already knows what's happening*
> *inside you, but he wants you to share*
> *honestly with him about your feelings.*
> *Wonderful things happen when you do.*

There were shepherds living out in the fields nearby, keeping watch over their flocks at night. An angel of the Lord appeared to them, and the glory of the Lord shone around them, and they were terrified. But the angel said to them, "Do not be afraid. I bring you good news that will cause great joy for all the people."

—LUKE 2:8–10 NIV

TWENTY-FOUR

Imagine Being Held by Jesus

My little boy nodded as though reporting nothing more remarkable than seeing a ladybug in the front yard. "Yeah, Jesus was there."

"Well, where was Jesus?"

Colton looked me right in the eye. "I was sitting in Jesus' lap."

—HEAVEN IS FOR REAL, XIX

Todd

It's no surprise to me that Colton's first memory of his trip to heaven is when he was sitting on Jesus' lap. Can you even imagine what that must have been like for him—going from a harsh, terrifying hospital operating room to the lap of the Son of God?

Picture those times when a young child, or even a pet, has run to you in terror, wanting to be protected from some scary thing. Safely nestled in your arms, the little one turns back and looks at the "beast," and suddenly fear is replaced by curiosity and security. That's the kind of memory Colton must have had in heaven, tenfold. What a blessing.

But for me, the image of my little boy sitting in Jesus' lap brings mixed feelings. I love knowing Jesus welcomed my son into the safety of his arms. But at the same time, I remember where *I* was while Colton was sitting in Jesus' lap: I was hiding out in the empty hospital room, raging at God for bringing my son so close to death—furious at the very One who at that moment, unknown to me, was holding my son in his arms.

Quite a contrast, isn't it?

I'd like to tell you that since I found out what was going on while I was having my pity-party meltdown, I no longer rant and rave at God when things go wrong. But that wouldn't be true. I still get frustrated. And I get mad. But now I get mad at the circumstances and not at God.

Sure, I still cry out to God to intervene in those hard circumstances. He expects me to ask him to keep my family and my friends safe. But at the same time I try to remember that God has a plan for my life—a plan that ends in heaven—and whatever is happening to me right now is part of that plan.

Yes, I still get frustrated. I want to know how my current difficulty fits into God's big picture. It would make things so much easier to endure the challenge at hand, wouldn't it? But God's ways are not our ways, and until it's my turn to sit in Jesus' lap and feel that unimaginable peace and security, I'm trying to live my life with that image in mind.

People have asked Colton, "When you saw Satan, weren't you afraid?"

He answers, "Well, Satan is scary, but I wasn't afraid.

Jesus was just showing me an image of Satan. It's not like he was right there."

Colton knew he was seeing just an image, not Satan himself. He explains that and then adds, "Besides, Jesus was standing next to me. You're not afraid when he's right there."

Imagine yourself, whenever hard times hit, climbing into Jesus' lap and turning back to look at the thing that has caused you pain or fear. I'll bet things won't look so scary there.

He took the children in his arms, placed his hands on them and blessed them.

—MARK 10:16 NIV

TWENTY-FIVE

Connecting through Loss

*Then two months into the pregnancy, Sonja lost the baby,
and our misty-edged dreams popped like soap bubbles.
Grief consumed Sonja. The reality of a child lost, one we
would never know. An empty space where there wasn't
one before.*

—HEAVEN IS FOR REAL, 35

Sonja

I miscarried two months into my second pregnancy, on
June 20, 1998. Father's Day weekend.

We hadn't told many people I was pregnant, thank
goodness, so very few people had to be told of our loss.
There didn't seem to be any sense in announcing it. Besides,
I certainly didn't feel like talking about it. As a result, only
a handful of people knew it had even happened. We kept the
miscarriage mostly to ourselves.

That Father's Day weekend, when it became obvious
what was going on, I curled up into the fetal position, lay on

our bed, and wept. I wanted to stay there forever, giving in to my grief and letting my family and the rest of the world go on without me. Yes, I knew Todd was hurting too. Yes, I knew our almost-two-year-old, Cassie, needed her mommy. But that day, I couldn't seem to get through my own grief to think about anyone but myself and the baby I had lost.

One of the hardest things about a miscarriage is just that: few people know or understand the grief that accompanies it. Many are quick to shrug it off, pat you on the shoulder, and say, "You'll be okay. You can always have another one."

People can easily understand the enormous loss parents feel when a child dies after being born, but it's harder for most to grasp the loss parents feel when they suffer a miscarriage.

Todd and I had probably never understood, ourselves, how much emotional pain a miscarriage can cause until we experienced it firsthand. And as hard as it is for prospective dads, there's an extra dimension of pain for the moms, because they can't help but wonder if they did something to cause it.

I certainly felt that way. I had tried to keep myself and the baby as healthy as I knew how. But something had gone terribly wrong, and I blamed myself for the baby's death. I prayed, asking God to forgive me for it, whatever *it* was.

And I asked God *why*? *Why* had our baby died?

I believe God is sovereign. I don't doubt that he has a bigger plan for my life than I can know this side of heaven. But that weekend it didn't really ease the pain of my loss to think that God had a reason for letting my baby die. Todd and I told ourselves God needed our baby for some other purpose than being our child. Frankly, we didn't like that, not one bit, but we accepted that belief.

A few months later, when I became pregnant with Colton,

we were ecstatic. But we were also scared, worrying that I would miscarry again. When he was born healthy, the joy and the relief we felt were indescribable.

Time passed, and as happens with most grief, our sorrow eased. But it never went away. Not by a long shot. Then, when Colton's appendix ruptured and it seemed we were going to lose him too, all the old grief came rushing back, along with the new terror that our son would die too.

It was so hard to understand how such pain and distress could be part of God's plan.

And then came the day, seven months after Colton's discharge from the hospital, that he told us he has *two* sisters: Cassie—and the sister who ran up to greet him when he visited heaven.

We were dumbfounded. And then comforted. So comforted that we knew we had to share what had happened. And in that sharing we began to see God's plan.

When a couple in our church endured a miscarriage, we reached out to them. We invited them into our home and shared their grief as only those who have experienced it can do. We cried with them and prayed with them. Then we told them what we believed: The baby we miscarried is in heaven. Colton saw her. That means your child is there too, we told them, and someday you're going to see him or her.

Over the years, we've walked through the grief of miscarriage with three other couples, and we've seen the impact our story has had on them. One of the moms told me, "Sonja, the one thing that helps me is knowing Colton saw his sister in heaven, so I know my baby is okay. It's tough now, but we're going to get through this because we have that hope that we'll see our child someday too."

We didn't bring that couple's baby back, but we journeyed through the freshest part of their grief with them and gave them hope. We also learned how powerful our story could be in helping others. To put it simply: that's why we wrote *Heaven Is for Real*.

Todd points out that when Jesus was urgently called to the home of his dying friend Lazarus, the Lord hung back for a few days. Lazarus and his two sisters were Jesus' friends, and they were also believers. They knew Jesus could save Lazarus from death. But Jesus didn't go, and Lazarus died. Still the Lord waited. Amazingly, he told his disciples, "I am glad for your sakes that I wasn't there" (John 11:15 MSG).

The disciples were confused. How could Jesus possibly be *glad* that his friend had died? He told them, "You're about to be given new grounds for believing."

You see, God doesn't do anything without a bigger purpose than we can imagine. But because we can't even begin to imagine it, we sometimes end up stuck in feelings of hurt and confusion.

Finally, after four days, Jesus and his disciples went to his friends' home. And what did Jesus do when he got to that sad place where Lazarus' sisters and their friends were mourning his death?

Jesus wept. That's right. He cried right along with his heartbroken friends.

At that point his disciples were probably *really* confused. After all, Jesus had told them he was glad Lazarus died. He had said he was going to use Lazarus' death to give them new grounds for believing. And yet there he was, weeping.

That's the kind of confusion you feel when you're a

believer and God lets something happen that turns your world upside down and breaks your heart.

It's what happened to us when I miscarried. Then it happened again when Colton almost died.

When you're that hurt and confused, you can end up curled in the fetal position, so grief-stricken you cannot function. Or in a closed-off hospital room, railing at God while your little boy undergoes emergency surgery with no assurance he'll live through it.

You think, *This isn't fair, Lord! We're following you! Why are you letting this happen to us?*

But that's when we need to remember Jesus' words: he may be using our difficult situation to provide "new grounds for believing."

After all, what did Jesus do in front of Lazarus' tomb? He called to him, "Lazarus, come out!" And Lazarus did!

Do you think any people in that crowd of friends and neighbors standing around the tomb might have become believers that day? Of course they did!

There are things God allows to happen because he knows the outcome is going to be greater than anything we could ever do on our own.

I've been criticized for saying God needed my unborn baby. But how can anyone look at the outcome and not believe that? I would never want to go through another miscarriage. Ever. But we've heard from hundreds, maybe thousands of people who have lost a child and who now are finding peace because they believe that child is in heaven and they will see him or her someday.

It's the part of Colton's story that has connected us most powerfully with hurting people around the world.

When I'm speaking somewhere to a women's group, I know that sharing our miscarriage experience is the thing that will most closely connect my heart to the hearts of many women in that audience. As a matter of fact, I have to brace myself for the reaction I've learned to expect. It's a subconscious reaction of hurt and heartache, and when I see it on a woman's face, I feel an instant connection, my heart to hers, sensing without asking that she too has lost a child.

Most recently, I saw that reaction during a tour of speaking appearances in the Midwest. If you were in one of those audiences, I want you to know I saw you.

Maybe you were that woman in the gray sweater. Or the lady wearing the pretty scarf. Or the older lady dabbing at her eyes with a tissue. I saw the pain in your faces as we shared the hurt in our hearts.

My prayer is that by sharing Colton's story I can reassure those women, and all parents who've lost a child, that they will see their little one again. Heaven is for real, and if my baby is there, so is yours. Everywhere we go, Todd and I tell people that giving people this kind of hope is why we wrote the book. It's why we do what we do.

Couples who have miscarried still seek out Todd for counseling. They know he understands because we've been where they are. We know how bad it hurts.

But now we have something else to share with them besides their grief.

Now we have hope.

Don't ever forget: Jesus controls life's outcomes. The greatest outcome might be one that only he can see today, but you will one day be able to see too! Heaven is waiting.

The Spirit also helps in our weaknesses. For we do not know what we should pray for as we ought, but the Spirit Himself makes intercession for us with groanings which cannot be uttered. . . . And we know that all things work together for good to those who love God, to those who are the called according to His purpose.

—ROMANS 8:26, 28

TWENTY-SIX

Waiting at Heaven's Gates

"In heaven, this little girl ran up to me and wouldn't stop hugging me," [Colton] *said in a tone that clearly indicated he didn't enjoy all this hugging from a girl.*

—HEAVEN IS FOR REAL, 96

Todd

Let's face it: about the only thing that can provide any comfort when we lose a loved one is knowing we will see that person again.

Oh sure, that's not what they teach in counseling courses and psychology classes. When those classes deal with the subject of grief, they say families need funerals as a way to bring *closure.* For people who have no hope of heaven, that's the best they can do: they say good-bye, and that's it. All they have is memories.

If you don't know God, I guess you can fall for that lie. But let me tell you, closure is man's plan, not God's. God has a much better plan. His plan is all about *reunion,* not closure.

If you need a reminder of that, think of what Colton said happened to him when he arrived in heaven: "This little girl ran up to me, and she wouldn't stop hugging me."

It took us awhile to figure it out, but soon we realized that, without a doubt, the girl who came running up to Colton was his big sister, the baby we had lost through miscarriage years earlier.

What a beautiful picture of heaven. It's probably the image that has touched more hearts than anything else in Colton's story. It's also part of the answer to the question we've been asked over and over again: why do you think *Heaven Is for Real* has found such a large audience?

The fact is, pastors like me confuse people in church. We make heaven sound complicated. We use words people don't understand and ramble on with complicated preaching while folks fall asleep in the pews. But here's a little boy saying he went to heaven and met his sister there. The sister he didn't know he had. When you read his story, you probably responded the same way Sonja and I did when we figured out who he was talking about: *Wow*.

All of us who have the hope of heaven have imagined what it's going to be like to meet Jesus, as well as the joy of seeing beloved family members who have died. But consider this: it's not just those loved ones you've cherished most on earth you'll see but also some you may not have known you had! You may have siblings or other family members who died through miscarriage, abortion, or other tragedies that you don't know about.

Can you imagine the joy we'll feel at that reunion, the amazement we'll have to maybe see a much bigger family than we thought we had? One man told us he'd always thought of himself as an only child because he was the only baby his mother was able to carry full term. She had suffered five miscarriages. He told us, "When I read your book I bawled, realizing I have five brothers and sisters in heaven." Consider how many people's families are going to be bigger in heaven than they are down here!

Here's another thing I love thinking about as I picture the reunion I'll have in heaven. It's based on a detail about Colton meeting his sister that didn't make it into *Heaven Is for Real*. Colton told us that when the angels and Jesus took him to heaven, his sister was waiting for him at the gate. He met his great-grandfather, Pop, in the throne room of God, but even before he walked through heaven's gates, his sister was there waiting for him. Somehow she knew he was coming, and she came running out to meet him. Even though Colton wasn't crazy about being hugged by a girl, after she let him know she was his sister, he realized how important this particular girl was.

Colton's experience tells me that our daughter in heaven is aging; maybe by the time we get to see her, she'll be a young lady. My own personal belief is that we will all be in our prime in heaven. Think about it: Jesus was thirty-three when he left earth and returned to heaven. Pop was a glasses-wearing older man when he died, but when Colton saw him he was young and clear-sighted. Sonja was two months pregnant when she miscarried the infant we now know was our daughter, but Colton saw her as a little girl.

So as I've imagined, dreamed, and prayed, this is the picture that keeps being rewound in my mind about my heavenly home-going: as I'm being flown by the angels to heaven and walking the last few steps with Jesus, a young lady comes running to greet me. She looks like Cassie but is a little bit like Sonja too, her dark hair streaming out behind her as she runs to give her dad a hug. I don't think I'm going to have to look for her or try to find her. I believe she's going to be there to meet me.

It doesn't take a rocket scientist to know which plan, God's or man's, is the one I'm choosing. Forget closure. I'm looking forward to that reunion in heaven. And I know my daughter is eager for that day too. Colton has already told us, "She can't wait for you and Mom to get to heaven."

Colton may not have appreciated being hugged by that little girl, but I'm looking forward to it more than I can describe.

He is not the God of the dead, but of the living, for to him all are alive.

—LUKE 20:38 NIV

TWENTY-SEVEN

Unforgivable? No!

I glanced in the mirror and saw Sonja slip the X-ray film from the brown envelope and hold it up in the streaming sunlight. Slowly, she began shaking her head, and tears filled her eyes.

"We screwed up," she said, her voice breaking over the images she would later tell me were burned in her mind forever.

I turned my head back enough to see the three small explosions she was staring at. The misshapen blotches seemed huge in the ghostly image of Colton's tiny torso. Why did they seem so much bigger now?

"You're right. We should've known," I said.

—*Heaven Is for Real*, 29

Todd

A lot of us struggle to forgive ourselves for the mistakes we make—or think we make. Parents probably have the hardest time with those struggles.

If Colton had died, Sonja and I would no doubt have felt responsible. Yes, we were following the doctor's advice, but we would have felt guilty anyway, thinking our gut instincts as protective parents should have kept us from meekly going along with what just felt wrong to us.

So I understand when parents come to me and say they can never forgive themselves for what they did or didn't do. Maybe they aborted a baby. Maybe they were driving drunk and caused an accident that killed their child. Maybe they turned their back one quick instant, and something went terribly wrong.

And now they're asking me, "How can I ever forgive myself for what I did?"

For help in answering them, I look at Jesus' example. When people were thinking wrong, he would redirect their attention. For example, when the Pharisees attacked him for working on the Sabbath, instead of answering them directly, he shot back questions of his own: Who's Lord of the Sabbath? Is it wrong to do good on the Sabbath?

When a young mother comes to me and says, "I had an abortion. I know I can never be forgiven for that," I try to help her change her thinking.

I tell her, "You're right. Jesus says there *is* an unforgiveable sin."

Usually, for a second she pauses . . . maybe swallows hard . . . and says, "Really?"

Yes, I answer, Jesus says there is an unforgiveable sin, and guess what: it's *not* abortion. Jesus says the one unforgiveable sin is blasphemy against the Holy Spirit.

Now, blasphemy is a very complicated thing to explain, but let me assure you, abortion has nothing in common with blasphemy against the Holy Spirit. I tell that woman abortion is 100 percent completely forgivable.

Most of the time the mother will look up at me with a smile starting to appear on her face. "It is?" she says.

At that moment, when I can see she's beginning to have a glimmer of hope, I continue. I ask, Do you know who Paul was? He was an apostle. But not just any apostle. He *murdered* Christians—men, women, children, and lots of them, not just one or two. Have you done anything that bad?

No, she says. Then I see her smile grow a little bigger.

So there's the answer. If God forgave Paul, why wouldn't he forgive you for what you did? Have you asked him to do that?

Only the unwilling are unforgivable. Is there any sin in your life you think God doesn't want to forgive? Do you realize that the only thing between you and forgiveness is you?

Every kind of sin and slander can be forgiven, but blasphemy against the Spirit will not be forgiven.
—MATTHEW 12:31 NIV

TWENTY-EIGHT

"But I Had an Abortion . . ."

"Who told you I had a baby die in my tummy?" Sonja said, her tone serious.

"She did, Mommy. She said she died in your tummy."

—*Heaven Is for Real, 94*

Todd

Sonja and I have had our fair share of ups and downs. For me, the births of our children are some of the greatest highs I've ever lived. But, as it goes for most parents, our kids have also provided some of our most difficult struggles.

For us, those first struggles started with Cassie's delivery, which was a little frightening—at least for me. Not just because she was the first but also because they apparently used some cone-shaped device during delivery. Looking at my daughter's resulting cone-shaped head, I didn't know what to say to Sonja when she asked me if our daughter was okay.

Then she asked again: "Todd, is our daughter okay?!"

Now, I'm sure all the husbands reading this will understand what I'm about to say and they'll likely agree with me, but it seems my wife gets a lot louder when she feels the need to repeat herself.

It was tough! I was motioning to my daughter's pointy head and glaring at the nurse while she quietly tried to tell me something like, "It'll be back to normal in twenty-four hours or less. Don't worry."

Yeah, maybe, but I just wasn't ready to tell Sonja that our daughter was "okay" at that moment. Pastors aren't supposed to lie, remember, and I wasn't convinced I would be telling the truth.

So the nurse and I stuck a little pink stocking cap on Cassie's head and hoped that, with the drugs and all the other stuff going on, maybe Sonja wouldn't notice. Still, it was all I could do to resist the urge to try to squeeze my daughter's head back into shape.

I was thinking, *I thought all I had to be worried about was them dropping her on her head. No one warned me about* this!

Today Sonja and I can laugh about that moment, and if you ask anyone (except maybe Cassie's brothers), they will tell you that Cassie's head is just fine.

But what happened with our next child reminded us that not all pregnancies end in laughter and joy. Our next child never made it to delivery; in fact, our baby never made it past two months in her mother's womb.

It really hurt when Sonja miscarried, and you all surely know that I'm not just talking about the physical pain Sonja went through. It hurt both of us emotionally. It broke our hearts. We now had a hole in our lives made by a child we never even got to hold. Next to Colton's scary ordeal, the miscarriage was our second worst low ever. We didn't know how to bounce back. We prayed and we grieved, but it took a long time for the hurt to ease.

Eventually, with the news that we were expecting another little one, we gradually moved on. But I can't say we ever really healed.

Colton's birth brought us great joy. We had a son! But then, just a few years later came his life-threatening crisis that sent us plunging to the depths again. And then, a few months later, came Colton's stunning revelation that sent Sonja and me to our knees in amazed gratitude. He had met, hung out with, and been repeatedly hugged by his unborn, older sister in heaven.

Wow! Talk about our highest high. That was it!

Some of the joy we experienced at that moment has been passed on to many of the readers of *Heaven Is for Real* who now have the same promise we do, that they will see their miscarried child someday in heaven.

Miscarriage has broken a lot of hearts in this world. And let's face it, the Bible doesn't have much to say about this terrible pain that some parents must deal with. It is completely silent on the most important question of all: *What happens to the baby?*

We know King David was comforted when his baby died after Bathsheba delivered him. His reassuring statement about going to his child one day (2 Samuel 12:23) has ultimately given hope to many parents who have lost children after they've been born.

There are many verses that talk about children in the womb. But where are the words of encouragement and hope for the parents who have *lost* unborn children? I haven't found them. And let me assure you, I've looked—no doubt like other parents who have suffered a miscarriage have looked too.

That's one of the reasons I believe many suffer through a miscarriage in silence, even those in the church. Jesus says, "Trust in me." And Sonja and I and many other Christians do. But we wished we could read a Bible verse from God that says specifically, "I've got your baby."

That's why, when Colton told us he'd seen his unborn sister in heaven, it was exactly what we needed. We had dreamed, prayed, questioned, but we finally had confirmation. Our baby—and not just our baby, our daughter (we hadn't known if it was a girl or boy)—is alive! And, according to Colton, she can't wait for us to get there too. That confirmation has been simply awesome for us.

Colton's story has healed many other wounded hearts like ours. But at the same time, I've found that his message of hope has also stirred up another pain in many parents' hearts. That hurt was first revealed when a middle-aged woman asked me a heart-wrenching question during a speaking appearance after *Heaven Is for Real* was published.

I've been asked many questions since the book was written, but this woman's question was one of the most difficult. It started with, "But I had an abortion . . ." followed by lots of tears. Then, as though the words could barely be spoken, she added softly, "I know God can forgive me for what I did. But will my *child* ever be able to forgive me for what I did?"

To be honest, I was so stunned by her question, I didn't know how to answer her. I hugged her, cried with her, prayed for her and prayed for myself, asking God to give me the right answer for her question.

I didn't have it then, but I believe now I do have the words I wish I could have said to that mom. (I don't know her name; I hope she will have the chance to read them here.) From the bottom of my heart, and after many hours on my knees, I believe the answer to her question is a resounding *yes!* Your child *will* be able to forgive you.

Let me tell you why.

Jesus came to earth to reconcile us to God, or, as Colton calls him, "his Dad." *Reconcile* means to make things right between two persons. Jesus came to earth and died in your place to make things right between you and his holy Dad.

Now, think about it: no one could have higher standards and greater expectations than a holy God, right? God has never wrongfully done anything to anyone. He's given grace. He speaks the truth. He always wants the best. He's never sinned against anyone. How do you meet the expectations of a God like that? You can't.

Which is why we need Jesus.

Jesus himself met all the requirements necessary to bring us back into a loving relationship with a holy God—in spite of all the terrible things in our lives, our pasts, and in our hearts. Jesus overcame *all* of our obstacles so he can present you and me blameless to the most exacting and particular Person of all—his holy Dad.

If you can accept that Jesus has made things right between you and God, you can surely believe that, by comparison, it's a piece of cake for him to make things right between you and your child. That means this same Jesus who will present you blameless and right to his Dad will also present you blameless and right to your aborted child.

Your child won't be questioning you when you meet him

or her. She won't be hurting. He won't be demanding. He or she will just be eagerly waiting to meet you face to face.

So here's the bottom line: no matter what circumstances surround the loss of your child, whether that baby was miscarried naturally or aborted unnaturally, all parents who trust in Jesus will have an amazing reunion with their unborn children in heaven.

If Jesus can reconcile you and your sinful past with our holy God, why would you doubt that he hasn't also made things right between you and your child?

If anyone is in Christ, he is a new creation; old things have passed away; behold, all things have become new. Now all things are of God, who has reconciled us to Himself through Jesus Christ, and has given us the ministry of reconciliation, that is, that God was in Christ reconciling the world to Himself.

—2 Corinthians 5:17–19

TWENTY-NINE

Urgent!

Colton pointed to the casket. "What's that, Daddy?"

I tried to keep it simple. "That's the casket. The man who died is inside it."

Suddenly, Colton's face gathered into that same knot of intense concern. He slammed his fists on his thighs, then pointed one finger at the casket and said in a near shout, "Did that man have Jesus?!"

Sonja's eyes popped wide, and we both glanced at the sanctuary doorway, terrified the family inside could hear our son.

"He had to! He had to!" Colton went on. "He can't get into heaven if he didn't have Jesus in his heart!"

—HEAVEN IS FOR REAL, 58–59

Todd

Soon after Colton visited heaven, he turned four, an age where, if something popped into his head, he'd just blurt it out. Like the time I took him to a restaurant and a guy with really long hair walked in, and Colton asked loudly whether that was a boy or a girl.

The thing is, four-year-olds are notoriously honest. What they blurt out is probably what everyone else is thinking but has the maturity *not* to say out loud.

I was preaching the funeral of a man I didn't know when Colton became obsessed with knowing whether or not the man knew Jesus. The fact was, I didn't know. And I don't think the man's family knew either. But they had asked me to do a funeral service for him, and as a courtesy I obliged.

The thing that's hard to write is not only what Colton said that day but *how* he said it. He seemed desperate, almost frantic. We tried to talk to him about having good manners, and he wouldn't get quieter. We tried to talk to him about respect, and he would not be silenced. It was like he was screaming at the top of his lungs: DAD! THIS MATTERS MORE THAN THE OTHER THINGS THAT YOU SAY MATTER!

Where did my little boy get such conviction that he was actually standing up to me when I was asking him to tone it down? Somehow Colton felt that being quiet was the wrong thing to do, and I had to wonder where he got such determination—to stand up to his daddy *in church*?

At the time I didn't know. But I found out later that Colton's strong conviction came from Jesus himself. Not from a Sunday school teacher, not from me. His conviction came from Jesus, who explained to him that he is the doorway to heaven.

It's one of the things that Jesus says about himself in the Bible (John 10:9). He says he's the door to heaven. It's really a bold statement, if you think about it. It's either right or it's wrong. There's no in between. He calls heaven his Dad's house (well, in John 14:2 KJV he says, "my Father's house"). Isn't that a great way to think of heaven? As God's *house*.

Jesus was giving us an image we all can understand. Just like any house down here on earth has a door, so does God's house—heaven. Jesus is that door.

Now let me ask you a question: Who do you welcome into your house? Does just anyone come through your front door and make himself or herself at home, cooking your food, sitting on your sofa, sleeping in your bed, using your remote? I'm guessing the answer is no. Houses don't work that way on earth.

When people want to come to my house, they knock on my door. I meet them there. Some I talk to and invite in. Most of the people I invite in are folks I already know. Or Sonja or our kids know them. My children are always bringing their friends into our house, and that's okay. I know they're my kids' friends.

God's house, heaven, works pretty much the same as your house. He says if you know his Son and have a relationship with him on earth, then he is more than welcome to bring you into his house.

I've been to many cities and towns, small and large, and never in a million years would I just walk up to someone's house I didn't know, open the door, and make myself at home. If I do know the person, I knock on the door and expect him or her to meet me, verify that we're friends, and then invite me in. But if I just walked up to the home of someone I didn't know and went right on in, I expect dire consequences would result. Alarms would probably go off; police would be called.

Unfortunately, some people have no better plan than that for going to heaven. They have no prior relationship with God, and they don't understand why they can't expect to just come on in.

Interviewers ask me if I believe what Colton said—if I believe you can't get into heaven if you don't have Jesus in your heart.

I just tell them it makes pretty good sense to me, because that's what Jesus said (John 14:6), and because that's how life works down here on this side of heaven.

But I'm quick to point out that the door to heaven swings open wide. Anyone who will invite Jesus into their house, their heart, is in turn welcome to Jesus' Dad's house in heaven. If you bring Jesus into your life and follow him, you can follow him right on into heaven.

I can tell you this: Colton is just as passionate today as he was nine years ago that you have to have Jesus in your heart in order to go to heaven. He found the door to heaven, and now he points the way to others. It's constantly on his heart and in his thoughts and prayers. He wants people to know Jesus because he knows that when they find him, they also find so much more.

At the end of a national TV interview in 2011, Colton was asked to close the segment by praying for those listening. That prayer wasn't rehearsed. It wasn't something he wrote down earlier and read in front of the cameras. It was spontaneous. Read the prayer now and again when you finish the book. If you don't know Jesus, Colton was, and is, praying that prayer for you.

Dear Father God,

*I just hope all those people out there who
haven't found you yet, or need to be reinforced
by your Word, Lord, just please help them so
that they may be able to come closer to you,
so that one day they may receive the gift that
you have given them. And Lord, I wish that,
even though we have a lot of people out there
who might not believe this, I just hope you
bless them so then they will figure out that you
are real, you are God. In Jesus' name. Amen.*

*I am the door. If anyone enters by Me, he will be
saved, and will go in and out and find pasture. . . .
In My Father's house are many mansions; if it
were not so, I would have told you. I go to prepare
a place for you. . . . Jesus said to him, "I am the
way, the truth, and the life. No one comes to the
Father except through Me."*

—John 10:9, 14:2, 6

THIRTY

Is Your Light On?

The wife of a pastor at a church in Colorado had once told me about something her daughter, Hannah, said when she was three years old. After the morning service was over one Sunday, Hannah tugged on her mom's skirt and asked, "Mommy, why do some people in church have lights over their heads and some don't?"

—HEAVEN IS FOR REAL, 74

Todd

I believe that the natural and spiritual worlds coexist, but most of us see only the natural one. Colton said that in heaven he could see a light above everyone's head, and later I was told what Hannah Goss, then three years old, had asked her mom, Barb, after church one Sunday morning. She posed a simple, straightforward question to her mother: "Why do some people at church have lights over their heads and some don't?"

What Hannah and Colton both saw points to an event

in the book of Acts. The Bible says when the Holy Spirit arrived at Pentecost tongues of fire came to rest on people's heads. For that moment, adult human beings were allowed to see into the spiritual world. It's possible they saw something that matches what both Hannah and Colton could see as children many years later.

We know the Holy Spirit remained with the apostles, but the Bible only records people seeing those tongues of fire on that one special day. But if the Holy Spirit didn't leave the apostles' hearts, isn't it also possible that the lights didn't go out above their heads either? Maybe their earthly eyes just weren't allowed to see the spiritual lights any longer.

Hannah, now an eighteen-year-old college student, can no longer see the lights above people's heads, but she hasn't forgotten the time she could. Her glimpse of something spiritual stays with her.

Of course, the first thing I asked Barb when I heard this story was if Hannah had seen a light above her mom's head. If I had found myself in that conversation with a child, my first instinct would have been to check. I would have raised my hand, pointed above my head, and asked the scary question: "Do you see a light here?" I would have wanted to know!

Barb admits she was too afraid to ask. It's kind of like going to the doctor when you think you might have cancer. Some people want to know, and some don't. The diagnosis can be too scary to face.

Did I mention that Barb is a pastor's wife? Still, asking if there was a light above *her* head was downright scary. Which confirms that point we often make: pastors and pastor's families are normal. We are not super-spiritual. And in that moment, Barb went with her gut reaction. She didn't ask.

Now, I'm not saying that Barb didn't know for sure that the Holy Spirit was in her life. You sure don't have to see lights above your head to be assured the Holy Spirit is in your heart. But I *will* say that I asked Hannah, "Did you see a light above your mom's head?"

Hannah answered with something like, "Of course!"

I was glad to get to break the news to Hannah's mom. "Guess what," I said. "There was a light above your head too!"

Barb shouldn't have had to wait for me to break the news. She could have known immediately, during that very first conversation. All she had to do was ask. But she didn't.

Most of us have a tendency to put off or avoid some very important issues in life. Even with today's advancements in medicine, we're told repeatedly that early diagnosis is one of the greatest tools doctors need for treatment. In fact, many diseases or health risks can *only* be treated if an early diagnosis is made. Many times, doctors can do nothing to help patients after the window of opportunity for treatment is gone. "If only we had known sooner" is a gut-wrenching statement to hear from your doctor.

It turns out the spiritual and the physical worlds have a lot in common. Sometimes, deep inside ourselves, we know something is wrong with our spiritual life, but we're afraid to find out what it is. I know people who attend church regularly but don't show any of God's light in their lives. I don't need a child to tell me that some people who are going through the motions of a religious life don't have a light shining above their heads or in their hearts.

Some people find real faith; others try to live off the faith of others. Some have had a personal experience with God; others only follow tradition and routine. Some have asked for forgiveness and have invited God's Spirit to come into their lives and are walking daily with God; others don't know God and are still trying to be "good enough."

Unfortunately, many cannot tell the difference in these two "diagnoses." If God is missing from your life, religious activity could be misunderstood as being "good enough." After all, you can't miss something you've never had.

Even people who do have God in their lives need constant spiritual check-ups. Regardless of the habits and hurts God has set us free from, this world continually invites us to return to our old godless habits. If we aren't watching, we can fall into relationships and behaviors that can devastate ourselves and our families.

Just because our relationships and loved ones are safe today, that doesn't mean they will be safe tomorrow without God's guidance or interruption. For the sake of yourself and all the people you care about, you deserve to know the truth right now. You need a diagnosis!

One of the synonyms for truth in the Bible is the word *light*. People who discover the truth are like people who step out of the darkness into the light. So let's move toward God's light together. You can take the first step by praying this prayer with me:

"God, is there something in my life that is going to hurt me or the people I love if you and I don't take care of it today? Please open my eyes to see what I need to fix, and give me the courage and the strength to do it now. Amen!"

*You deserve to know the truth
about yourself—right now.*

*He who does the truth comes to the light, that his
deeds may be clearly seen, that they have been
done in God.*

—JOHN 3:21

THIRTY-ONE

The Coach's Challenge

I remember seeing my mother in anguish at the funeral, but her grief didn't end there. As I got older, I'd sometimes catch her in prayer, with tears gently sliding down her cheeks. When I asked her what was wrong, she would share with me, "I'm worried about whether Pop went to heaven."

—*HEAVEN IS FOR REAL*, 89

Todd

I'm a small-town guy, and that means I wear a lot of different hats. It's what small-town people do. I'm a pastor and a businessman. (I still work for the garage-door company I used to own.) I'm also a volunteer firefighter and still love to coach wrestling. Sometimes I switch hats so many times during the day it's hard to keep track of which one I'm wearing at any particular time. They all blend together. Those of you who live in rural America know that's how small towns work. It might seem strange to city people, but to small town folk, this lifestyle is normal.

Right now I'm wearing my coach's hat. So this message is primarily for the men who may be reading this book. Women, it's okay if you read what I say here; it's possible it might apply to you too. But in my experience, this message needs to be heard by men.

Pop, my maternal grandfather, was a good, hard-working man. He went to church every now and then, and he talked about the typical things men discussed in those days. Growing up, I knew he'd be at the doughnut shop most mornings to meet his buddies and talk about whatever was going on in town or on the farm—crops, the weather, someone's new truck, things like that. But he never brought up his faith, at least not to my mom. Never talked about spiritual things. So when he died, he left my mom (his daughter) wondering. And not just musing idly about his eternal destination but worrying and fretting so sorrowfully that it impacted her life for years after he died.

All unnecessarily.

Some of you men reading this are all too much like Pop. I'm not questioning if you love your families or not. I'd just like to ask you . . . how much?

Here's how things could have been for my mom as she grieved for her dad. I recently buried a friend named Wilfred. It's always hard to preach a friend's funeral, but Wilfred's funeral was the opposite of how Pop's funeral unfolded all those years ago. Like Pop, Wilfred was a hard-working man, fiercely loyal to his family, and a good provider. A few months ago, Wilfred had to undergo open-heart surgery. Before the operation, he pulled me aside to talk, and he said, "Todd, I want you to know this: I've told my kids and my wife that everything is okay between me and God." (Wilfred was a member of my congregation and many times had heard me give this same challenge I'm now sharing with you.)

Wilfred made it through the surgery, and we began to pray hard for his recovery. (In the next chapter we share how our son Colby prayed for Wilfred.) For sixty days, we thought God was answering our prayers, and we expected Wilfred would soon be back among us, resuming his busy life. But then he died, and as his pastor, I was called upon to preach his funeral.

Was the funeral sad? Yes. Everyone cried, including the pastor preaching the sermon. Do we miss Wilfred? Yes, every day. But while we mourn our loss, because we can't help but miss this friend who meant so much to us, nobody has to ask where Wilfred is. We all know. Most importantly, his family knows. Because he had told them.

Wilfred's funeral was what Christian funerals are supposed to be: a celebration of a life well lived. Yes, and also a time for loved ones to mourn. But that funeral was completely different from Pop's—and so many others'—because each of Wilfred's immediate family members had been told *by Wilfred,* not their pastor, that Wilfred was square with God. He had been forgiven, he'd given his life to Jesus, and things were good between Wilfred and God.

I didn't have to reassure anybody. Wilfred had already done it. He had manned up. He'd had that discussion with his family, and as a result they had unwavering assurance and confidence about where he was spending eternity. It was the best gift Wilfred could give to his family—one that I, as pastor, never could have given them.

Men, if you ask your wives if they'd like you to talk with

them about your faith, what do you think they will say? (And if the shoe is on the other foot, then women, consider this question directed at you with regard to your husband.) If you're hesitant to ask, then let me be her voice for a minute. Let me speak for your kids and grandkids and your closest friends: *yes,* they would love for you to tell them you're square with God and that you have accepted Jesus as your Lord. Believe me, it's a lot more reassuring coming from you now than when it comes at your funeral from some pastor who may or may not know you. They need to hear it from *you.*

My mom needed to hear it from her dad, but Pop didn't tell her. In his defense, a reasonable man would have thought he had time. Pop didn't know he was going to be killed in an accident two days after he made that decision.

So the years passed, and my mom wondered and worried whether she would see her dad again in heaven. Only when Colton came back from heaven and told us he'd met Pop there did we know for sure. *Then* we learned from a relative that Pop had attended a special service in a little country church just two days before he died and had quietly raised his hand when the preacher asked, at the end of the sermon, if anyone wanted to give his life to Christ.

Because he didn't tell his family, Pop left his family, including his daughter (my mom) wondering if she would ever see her dad again. So she spent twenty-eight long years not knowing about her father's decision that night.

What a difference Pop could have made by coming home from that little church, gathering his family around him, and happily saying, "I want to tell you something . . ."

What comfort he could have given them.

Let me tell you, peace at a funeral is a precious thing.

And let me tell you something else that I've learned from firsthand experience: the deceased person can give his or her family way more peace than any pastor ever can.

Men are taught to take care of their families, to buy life insurance and make other financial arrangements so their loved ones will be okay if the husband-dad dies first. But something much more important than life insurance is the confidence of knowing you're right with God. Man up! Tell them! Give them that gift.

And if you *haven't* asked God for forgiveness and accepted Jesus into your heart, take care of that—*now* would be a good time—and then have that talk with your family.

> *It's not your pastor's job to give your family peace at your funeral. It's yours. So man up! Take care of that responsibility right now.*

The jailer called for lights, rushed in and fell trembling before Paul and Silas. He then brought them out and asked, "Sirs, what must I do to be saved?"
They replied, "Believe in the Lord Jesus, and you will be saved —you and your household." Then they spoke the word of the Lord to him and to all the others in his house. At that hour of the night the jailer took them and washed their wounds; then immediately he and all his household were baptized. The jailer brought them into his house

*and set a meal before them; he was filled with joy
because he had come to believe in God—he and
his whole household.*

—ACTS 16:29–34 NIV

THIRTY-TWO

Contagious Faith

When, in the spring of 2004, the most brilliant rainbow we'd ever seen appeared over Imperial, we called him outside to take a look....

Colton was down the hall in the playroom. "Hey, Colton," I called. "Come out and take a look at this."

He emerged from the playroom and joined us on the front stoop.

"Look at that rainbow, Colton," Sonja said. "There definitely should be a big pot of gold at the end of that thing."

Colton squinted, peering up at colors pouring across the sky.

"Cool," he said with a nonchalant smile. "I prayed for that yesterday."

Then he turned on his heel and went back to play.

—HEAVEN IS FOR REAL, 108–109

Sonja

When Colton prayed for a rainbow and wasn't at all surprised when one appeared the next day in spectacular fashion, his siblings (and his parents) were watching—and learning. Now Colton's little brother Colby fully expects his specific prayers to be answered too. Obviously, Colton's attitude has rubbed off on his little brother—and on a lot of other people too.

Colby is a typical little brother to Colton and Cassie: fiercely loyal one minute and an annoying pest the next. It's normal in our house to hear Colton and Colby arguing over some injustice one of them committed (at least in the other brother's eyes). Usually it's that one of them has "borrowed" the other one's something-or-other without asking.

But despite their occasional spats and the differences in their ages and personalities, one of the things that's become most apparent to us as Colby gets older is that he has "caught" his big brother's childlike faith.

What we saw happening in Colby, we wanted to see happen in other kids as well. We asked ourselves, what if other kids, not only Colby, could catch Colton's simple, childlike faith? That's how the children's book *Heaven Is for Real for Kids* came about. As we started writing it, our goal was that children would learn what Colton already understands and that they would "catch" his contagious faith and then pass it on.

We worked hard to put Colton's experience into a story that was appealing and understandable to children. The book was published, and we began hearing from many families that it had become a favorite with their kids. But nothing prepared us for a video the Thudium family sent us of their seven-year-old son, Graham, "reading" *Heaven Is for Real for Kids* to his church congregation, something he had asked to do. (Actually, Graham's dad said Graham had memorized the book, so we don't know if he was actually reading the words as the pages were turned or reciting it from memory.)

Graham was in the end stages of his battle against an inoperable brain tumor, so his speech was distorted. His dad repeated each line after Graham said it first. It seems impossible that anyone could watch the video without tears—or without being fully convinced that Graham "caught" Colton's faith and was eager to pass it on. I can't imagine anyone watching the video (youtube.com/watch?v=8UcJk9DQuZg) without tears, and without being inspired about the truth that heaven is for real. Graham's faith is contagious too.

Two days after Todd watched this video, he contacted Graham's family, only to learn that Graham had entered heaven just moments earlier. Todd wept with his dad at the loss of their child, but at the same time we are all comforted that Graham and his family faced Graham's death knowing exactly where he would be the moment he sighed out that last breath. And we rejoice to imagine that day when Graham's parents will see their boy again in heaven, healthy, whole, and cancer-free. We plan to see him there too!

A kid's faith is contagious. Not only do kids "catch" the gift of personal faith from each other, including their siblings, they also spread it to the adults who are fortunate enough to hear them.

*Don't ever forget: some contagious
things, like faith, are worth catching.*

*In Christ Jesus you are all children of God through
faith.*

—GALATIANS 3:26 NIV

THIRTY-THREE

A Child's Prayers

One of the great blessings of our lives as parents has been listening to our kids pray. When they are small, children pray without the showiness that sometimes creeps into our prayers as grown-ups, without that sort of "prayer-ese," a language meant to appeal more to anyone listening than to God. And when Colton and Cassie offered prayers in their plain, earnest way, it seemed that God answered.

—HEAVEN IS FOR REAL, 124

Sonja

When *Heaven Is for Real* became a *New York Times* best seller, Todd and I didn't know what to think of it. When it stayed at the top of the best-seller list, we *really* didn't know what to think! But we vividly remember the day when Colby, then about four, came into the room and announced in a very Colton-like way, "I know why *Heaven Is for Real* is number one."

We tuned in, wondering what he was going to say.

"It's because of me," he said. "Well, God too. But I've been praying for that. That's why the book's number one."

While Colton is our rather quiet, sensitive, matter-of-fact child, Colby, now seven, is our family comedian—and also our family inspiration when it comes to having an amazing prayer life.

I pray with Colby at bedtime (I prayed with Colton and Cassie too when they were young, but now that they're older they pray on their own). One night, as Colby and I prayed together, he remembered that we had prayed earlier that day as a family, asking God to give us just the right words to say in an upcoming national television interview. That night, Colby prayed that Colton would "do good" in the interview. And I have to tell you, the next day, when the host of the Christian TV program turned to Colton and, without having mentioned it to him beforehand, asked him to pray to close the interview, Colton absolutely knocked it out of the park. (It's the prayer we share on page 139 and at the end of the book.) He prayed confidently but humbly, asking God to reach the unbelievers. It was a short but powerful prayer that basically left all of us breathless.

When we called home and told Colby and Cassie about it, Colby had his usual answer ready: "I prayed for that."

All his life, Colby has seen his parents and siblings praying, but I think it's been Colton's prayers that have influenced him most. Colby has the sweetest, closest conversations with God. I think of adults who are shy about praying aloud in front of others, and I wish they could have the innocent attitude toward prayer that Colby has.

He understands, though, that God doesn't always

answer our prayers the way we hope. When our friend Wilfred underwent heart surgery, Colby took full credit for his surviving for sixty days following the surgery because he had prayed for him nearly every night.

But then came the day when Wilfred died. We dreaded telling Colby but knew we had to. Finally I took him aside, knelt down in front of him and said, "Colby, Jesus took Wilfred to heaven."

His shoulders sagged, and he looked sad but didn't say anything. We didn't know how he was processing the news, but at prayer time that night we sat down together, and he said, "Mom, can I pray first?"

"Sure," I said. "Go head, Colby."

He bowed his head, put his hands together and said, "God, I just pray you give Wilfred a really good time in heaven."

Then he looked at me. "Okay, Mom, your turn," he said.

I couldn't speak. Everything I would have said, Colby had summed up in those few, faith-filled words.

"Mom? Your turn."

"I can't."

"You have to. It's your turn."

I couldn't trust my voice not to break. All I could squeak out without sobbing was to say, "What Colby said, Jesus. Amen."

Sometimes we wonder if our kids can understand what we may think are adult situations beyond their comprehension—like a Christian friend's death even though we prayed he would live—when in fact the kids may be way ahead of us. That was certainly the case when Wilfred died. While all of us adults were stuck in our earthly grief, Colby was already picturing our friend's arrival in heaven and asking God to show him a good time.

Sometimes adults think they have to speak in flowery "prayer-ese" when they're praying. But I'm convinced that our children's simple prayers fall as sweetly on God's ears as they do on ours. We should all speak so simply—to each other and to God!

As an example, Colby recently prayed for another friend—an elderly church member, Ruby, whose vision has been failing, causing her to suffer some falls. One night as we knelt together by Colby's bed, he prayed, "Dear Jesus, please keep Ruby's heart beating so she stays alive, and help her when she falls down. She's been falling down a lot lately, Jesus, and I don't want her to get hurt."

Children's prayers are precious and powerful, full of the simplest and purest joy, love, and faith.

If you're one of those people who have a hard time putting voice to your prayers, let your young children's prayers be your guide.

Jesus said, "Let the little children come to me, and do not hinder them, for the kingdom of heaven belongs to such as these."
                                        —MATTHEW 19:14 NIV

THIRTY-FOUR

A Perfectly Normal Pastor's Family Is Imperfect

As for Colton, he'll turn eleven this month and in September will enter the sixth grade. He's a regular kid in every way.

—HEAVEN IS FOR REAL, 154

Sonja

As we write this book, Colton's still a "regular kid," and now he's a teenager. Which means that, like every teenager, he has his faults and eccentricities. He is very matter-of-fact and precise. When I'm away from home and call to ask him what time he went to bed the night before, he may say, "Nine thirty-one." Not "around nine thirty," not "a little before ten," but "nine thirty-one."

It makes me laugh. It's one of his endearing qualities that we've seen all his life. Throughout the years since he started telling us about his visit to heaven, if we said anything that didn't quite jive with what he had seen or experienced there, he was quick to correct us. Like the time Todd asked Colton what he did in heaven "when it got dark."

Colton wasn't having it. He said, "It doesn't get dark in heaven, Dad! Who told you *that*?"

If only he could be so particular about his household chores! But no, he's an ordinary teenager, pushing the envelope occasionally. Not long ago, I got suspicious about the condition of his clothes. Todd and I want our kids to grow up learning to be independent, so as soon as they are ten years old, they do their own laundry. At least once a week, they either wash, dry, and put away their own clothes, or they go naked or stink. Those are the choices.

At least that's how it's supposed to work. But a year or so ago I wasn't seeing any evidence that Colton was doing his laundry. A week went by, and there were no Colton clothes in the laundry room. Another week, and still nothing.

Finally I asked Colton, "What's the deal with your laundry? Have you washed your clothes?"

He assured me all was well: "I've got it covered, Mom."

Hmmm. That wasn't exactly the answer I was looking for.

"What do you mean you've got it covered? Have you washed your clothes?" I asked again.

"It's okay, Mom. I took care of it," he said confidently.

"Colton! *Have you washed your clothes?*"

"Mom, really. It's okay. I Axed everything."

"You *what*?!"

"I Axed it—you know, sprayed everything with Axe."

In case you don't have a teenage boy in your house, Axe is a men's body spray that's very trendy right now. Not exactly what moms have in mind as a substitute for washing a teenage boy's laundry.

That day Colton and his mother and a very large, stinky load of laundry had what we call in our house a "come to Jesus" moment: a session of confession, apology, and then action—in Colton's case, an afternoon spent doing his laundry.

Like I said, Colton's a regular kid. A good kid: polite, fun, strong in his faith, good musician, and a good athlete—but occasionally ornery too. He's a reminder to us that God uses ordinary people, and sometimes the least expected people, to do his work on earth.

Not that Colton can be compared with Jesus and the work *he* did, but, being the mother of two sons, sometimes I wonder about Jesus as a boy. The Bible tells us he was "fully human" (Hebrews 2:17 NIV)," and that makes me wonder if, as a youngster, he might have frustrated his mother, Mary, now and then—and I'm not just talking about the time he went missing as the family was traveling home with a crowd from Jerusalem and they later found him teaching in the temple. I'm wondering if there were times when he didn't carry in the water jugs when he was supposed to or maybe stayed too long at a friend's house, riding stick horses or climbing trees, or if he and his friends were caught playing on the riverbank when they'd been told not to go there without an adult.

When I get to heaven, I may just ask Mary, "Did Jesus ever get spanked or have to do a time-out?"

I know Jesus never sinned, but he was still a boy!

While moms and dads are always on the lookout for our kids' misbehaviors (and perhaps occasionally sniffing their gym clothes to see if they're being washed or Axed), I was reminded recently that we also need to keep an eye out for those thoughtful and helpful things they do as well. Another independence-training thing we practice in our family is that, as soon as our kids could read reasonably well, they started ordering for themselves when we eat out at a restaurant. Usually Todd and I order, and then the server may ask us "And the kids?"

Todd answers, "They'll order for themselves," and they do.

In our little town, the restaurants serve home-style food; it's not like the kids have to be able to read French or Italian or figure out some fancy menu descriptions. So it's not a problem for Cassie and Colton, but Colby, at seven, still needs help occasionally, especially if we go to a new place. What we hope he'll do is ask us, or ask the server, for help if there are words he can't figure out. But he wants to be a big guy, like his teenage siblings, so he usually sees that option as a last resort.

But recently a friend pointed out to us that when we're in a restaurant where Colby's not familiar with the menu, Colton will find out what Colby wants and then help him order it.

To be honest, this surprised me. I had just told this friend that Colton tended to pick on Colby, like some big brothers are known to do. That's when she reminded me what had happened when we had been in a Quizno's the day before. When we were in line, our friend Debbie pointed out that Colton told the order-taker, "And my brother will have . . ."

I had totally overlooked that little deed of kindness (probably remembering instead that Colton had made fun of Colby later for ketchup on his cheek or shredded cheese on his lap). But it was true. He did order for his younger brother.

Just as an aside to give you another glimpse into our ordinary family, I insisted that our kids write down three goals for the year. A couple of them wrote down that they would read their Bible every day. One of Colby's goals is to take a shower every day—a goal for which we're all thankful.

My point in writing this reading is to nudge you to look for the good in people, especially your kids, and also to remind you that the people around you—your friends and family members and even strangers—may be as "ordinary" as you are and yet, in God's eyes, they're special creations that he may be using to touch a life for good. That ordinary person doing God's work might even be *you*!

People like to be appreciated. Whose deed of kindness can you thank someone for before today ends? Who knows? It might be your child's.

She did an excellent thing for me. . . . I tell you the truth, wherever the Good News is preached in all the world, what this woman has done will be told, and people will remember her.

—MARK 14:6, 9 NCV

THIRTY-FIVE

"Dad, Jesus Told Me to Tell You"

No matter what new tidbits he revealed, though, Colton had one consistent theme: he talked constantly about how much Jesus loves the children. I mean that: constantly.

He would wake up in the morning and tell me: "Hey Dad, Jesus told me to tell you, he really loves the children."

Over dinner at night: "Remember, Jesus really loves the children."

Before bed, as I helped him brush his teeth, "Hey, Daddy don't forget," he'd say, garbling the words through a mouthful of toothpaste foam, "Jesus said he really, really loves the children!"

Sonja got the same treatment.

—HEAVEN IS FOR REAL, 105–106

Todd

Colton came back from heaven with an urgent message for me. Jesus had told him to tell us that he loves the children.

To be honest, if it had been anyone else sending us that message, I might have thought, *Duh! I know that. There are lots of places in the Bible where Jesus showed us how important children are to him.* But Colton's emphasis wasn't on the message. It was on *me*. This is how he said it: "*Dad*, Jesus told me to tell *you* he really loves the children."

Sonja has always had a huge heart for children's ministries. It's her passion. But when Colton came back from heaven with this message from Jesus directly to me, I had to take some time to consider just what Jesus wanted me to do with it.

While Sonja has been a kind of hands-on children's worker, I've been the one overseeing everything, if you want to put pastoring a church in business terms. The children's ministry was a part of my job, but it sure wasn't the priority.

But then came that personal message delivered by Colton, and I knew I needed to pray for guidance so I would know the best work to do in response to it. Gradually it became clear to me I couldn't be a preacher who focuses just on the adults.

Let me step back a minute and give you a little background. As I grew up, two preachers had very different influences on my life. I grew up in a small church with a weekly attendance of seventy to eighty, tops. The pastor of that church acted as if he was really important, so parents ran interference between him and the children in the church. We kids weren't supposed to "bother" him.

Then, when I was twelve, my family visited a church with more than a thousand people in attendance. The second Sunday we attended, I was standing by myself in the crowded foyer surrounded by more people than I'd ever seen anywhere. Suddenly someone called me by name and said, "Todd, I'd like to meet you."

It was the pastor of that huge church. I had no clue how he knew my name, but there he was, talking to me as though I was the most important person in the room. Several people came up, obviously wanting to talk to him, but he said, "Sorry, I can't talk to you right now. I'm talking to Todd."

When my parents saw the pastor talking to me, they thought, *Oh, no. What did he do?* (I have to admit, *alarm* was the more common response for them when they saw me being addressed by someone in authority.)

It's got to be obvious which pastor showed me that I mattered and made me feel special. As I thought about the message Colton brought to me from heaven, I knew God wanted me to be *that* kind of pastor.

It's not just being a preacher in a church that welcomes children. It's about everything that I am. I try to make kids feel special and important. We wrote the kids' version of *Heaven Is for Real* hoping to convince all the children who read it that they matter, and that Jesus *really* loves them.

Sonja and I have been all over the country since the book was published, making a point to speak to children's workers, encouraging them and urging them, "Don't quit. Don't give up. What you do is one of the most important things in the church today."

Sometimes I look at what has happened in the years since Colton visited heaven and came back to deliver the message from Jesus, and I think this must be how the apostle Peter felt when Jesus told him to get out of the boat and walk across the water to him. I'm doing something I never thought possible—spreading Jesus' message about kids on a global level.

Have you ever considered what message Jesus has for

you? If your child visited heaven, would he or she come back and say, "Mommy, Jesus really loves the people who are sick and dying and wants you to take care of them." Maybe hospice nurses hear that in their spirits.

Or, "Daddy, those people who work in your office are alone and hurting. He really loves them, but they don't know it."

Or, "Sister, Jesus told me to tell you the kids in your class, those girls who are always worried about what they wear, the guys who feel they can never be good enough, he really loves them."

Or, "Brother, Jesus told me to tell you to help with teenagers . . ."

Old people, children, the sick, the youth group, there are so many opportunities for carrying God's love to the world. The list could go on and on. Everyone's calling may be different, and each one is special.

Have you let God speak to you, get your attention?

When I prepare to receive my reward in heaven, I'm pretty sure Jesus is going to bring up the message he sent to me from Colton. Maybe it might sound something like this: "Well, Todd, Colton did his job. He told you what I told him to. Now what did you do with it?"

If Jesus loves you (and I promise you, he does), he wants to use *you* for something important too. Maybe you won't have such an obvious message as I did, with your four-year-old following you around the house harassing you. But God does want to get your attention. Does he have it yet? Jesus told Colton to tell me he really loves the children. And now I'm telling you he has a message for you too. What are you going to do with your message?

What has Jesus asked you to do?

*Before I shaped you in the womb, I knew all about
you. Before you saw the light of day, I had holy
plans for you.*

—JEREMIAH 1:5 MSG

THIRTY-SIX

Really Loving the Children

"And he really, really loves us, Dad. You can't belieeeeve how much he loves us!"

—*Heaven Is for Real*, 100

Sonja

When Colton told me again and again that Jesus loves the children, he was preaching to the choir. I've had a heart for children for a long time—about as long as I've had a heart! As a pastor's wife, I have many opportunities to serve the church (as all church members do), but if you come to church looking for me, you'll probably find me somewhere working with the kids.

I've been known to say, "Whatever is your passion, do it until you die." Well, my passion is helping kids, and as I speak to various groups I always begin by apologizing for not being a professional speaker and by admitting, "I'd rather be in the nursery right now, or in the Sunday school rooms, teaching the kids Bible stories, instead of up here talking about myself."

One of the gratifying things that has come about since *Heaven Is for Real* was published is that a lot of people have a new understanding of and appreciation for the importance of children's ministries. The Bible tells us several times how Jesus held children in very high regard. In fact, he said, "Unless you change and become like little children, you will never enter the kingdom of heaven" (Matthew 18:3 NIV).

Todd says that the part of Colton's story that has impacted him the most is when he asked where Colton sat in God's throne room and Colton answered, "They brought in a little chair for me."

That image was a wake-up moment for us that made everything else click. We suddenly understood that heaven is not a spiritual place where we'll float between the clouds. It's a physical, solid, tangible, real place where children are honored.

Think about it. In our church sanctuaries today we have seats and pews that are all one size—adult size. It's rare to find a church auditorium where there are child-sized pews or chairs.

Although I might wish it were different, that's true in our Nebraska church too. After all, most young kids sit with their parents during church services. Down in the basement where our children's classes are held, though, things are different. When we gather in the fellowship hall for church dinners, children have tables and chairs of their own, sized just right for them. And the Sunday school rooms have furniture in various sizes, depending on the age of the children it's intended for (though I have to fight to keep those little tables in place; they're way too convenient for other uses!)

When children come into those areas, they feel welcome.

Everything fits them, and they know it's "their" place. That's where I want to be when I'm in church, down there on the little chairs, working with the kids.

In many churches, children's ministries are understaffed, undersupplied, and have no prepared curriculum. Those programs are at the bottom of the barrel, and those who work in those ministries are often overworked and overwhelmed.

If you're one of them, if you're down there with me—whether you're sitting on the floor in a little church somewhere that can't afford special furniture for the kids or in a megachurch somewhere playing in a band for children's church when you'd rather be in the sanctuary worshipping with the adults?I want you to know that what you're doing is important. And it's not just me telling you that; it's Jesus.

I've heard some people say that churches with limited budgets (and most churches fall into that category) need to focus their funds on adult ministries because it's the adults who provide the money the church needs to survive. That's just wrong. They're forgetting that by investing in the kids, we're investing in the future of the church. When you teach Sunday school, you're planting in those little hearts the seeds of the gospel that they will carry with them throughout their lives, hopefully sharing it with others.

Who knows who those children may grow up to be? I've heard it said, "You may be the one who touches the one who changes the world." I like that.

Early in Todd's ministry, we led a youth group in Bartlesville, Oklahoma. We considered the participants so much like family that we referred to them as "our kids." Many of them are now in their thirties with children of their own. In the years that have followed, can you imagine how heartwarming it's been for us when some of them have asked Todd to officiate at their weddings? Or how encouraging it has been to us to hear that many of them are now in church leadership themselves somewhere? We are so happy that they continue to let us be a part of their lives. It tells us that the energy and love we put into those young people all those years ago has really paid off. It's a reward like no other.

Today we continue our emphasis on children in our current church. We want the kids to know they're valued—they *matter.* We consider them a fully accepted part of our congregation and that what we're doing is our service to the Lord.

As for the money part of it, our church's practice is not to pass an offering plate during services but to place offering boxes by the sanctuary doors. If people want to give, they can give as they pass by the box. Recently, we put up another offering box that is at kids' level. That little box tells the children their contributions are valued too, whether it's a penny or a dollar.

If this feels like a pep talk for children's workers, you're absolutely right. I want to be an encourager and supporter of children's ministry workers everywhere. As we've traveled around the country, it has warmed my heart to have people tell me that because of *Heaven Is for Real,* they've been motivated to keep on going as children's workers when they had been feeling as though they should just give up. Most of them admit that their passion, like mine, is kids. They say they felt unappreciated, or they felt like they weren't accomplishing anything. Then they've read Colton's story and remembered who *does* value what they're doing down there in the basement teaching Sunday school: *Jesus.*

And *that's* what matters most.

But you may feel differently. Maybe you're one of those church members who get annoyed by the noise that comes with children or you get offended by the stains they leave behind in a perfectly clean church. If that's you, I hope you'll have the courage to reconsider. To start, maybe you'll go to one of those marks on the wall or the stain on the brand-new carpeting and ask yourself this question: did Jesus die to save the carpet you're standing on or the kid who made the stain?

Write a note to the children's Sunday school teachers in your church, saying thank you. Or volunteer to help in your church's children's ministry.

People brought little children to Jesus for him to place his hands on them and pray for them. But the disciples rebuked them. Jesus said, "Let the little children come to me, and do not hinder them, for the kingdom of heaven belongs to such as these."

—MATTHEW 19:13–14 NIV

THIRTY-SEVEN

Seeing the Face of Jesus

Of the literally dozens of portraits of Jesus we'd seen since 2003, Colton had still never seen one he thought was right.

Well, *I thought,* may as well see what he thinks of Akiane's attempt.

I got up from the desk and hollered up the stairs for Colton to come down to the basement. . . .

"Take a look at this," I said, nodding toward the computer monitor. "What's wrong with this one?"

He turned to the screen and for a long moment said nothing.

"Colton?"

But he just stood there, studying. I couldn't read his expression.

"What's wrong with this one, Colton?" I said again.

Utter silence.

I nudged him in the arm. "Colton?"

My seven-year-old turned to look at me and said, "Dad, that one's right."

—Heaven Is for Real, 144–145

Todd

It's hard to describe the feelings I had that day when, after three years of showing Colton pictures of Jesus and having him reject them, a picture painted by a little girl we'd never met connected with him so strongly, without question, that it stopped him in his tracks.

A friend had sent me a three-minute CNN clip that told the story of a girl in Idaho, twelve years old at the time of the report, who had started having visions of heaven at age four. Her name is Akiane Kramarik, she's Lithuanian-American, and her descriptions of heaven, shared in the CNN 2006 report, included references to out-of-this-world colors and Jesus' extraordinarily beautiful eyes.

The really amazing thing, to me at least, was that at that time Akiane's parents were atheists, and God was never mentioned in their home. The family didn't watch television. Akiane was homeschooled. Yet she repeated her vivid descriptions of heaven so many times, first in words and then in paintings, that her mother, knowing Akiane couldn't have heard or seen these things anywhere else, believed she was spiritually awakened.

This time God wasn't speaking to the pastor's kid. He was speaking to the child of a nonbelieving family.

The CNN report included some of Akiane's beautifully detailed paintings, including a close-up of her portrait of Christ. I paused the video and called Colton to come and see it, and the sight of it stopped him cold.

He was six-going-on-seven by the time he saw Akiane's picture of Jesus. He'd rejected so many other pictures depicting how artists had imagined Christ's likeness that I expected him to discount this one too. But when I showed him the picture, he saw those striking, unforgettable eyes looking out at him again.

We got Akiane's (and her parents') permission to reproduce her picture, titled *Prince of Peace: The Resurrection,* in *Heaven Is for Real.* The response has been almost beyond comprehension. We've heard from parents who've told us about their children who had recovered from some kind of life-threatening experience or had seen visions and had begun telling stories similar to Colton's. Typically, the parents had read *Heaven Is for Real,* and they'd opened it to show Akiane's painting to their children. "That's him," the children would say. "That's Jesus. That's the one I saw in heaven."

A mom in North Platte told us her son Jeremiah had had eye surgery the day after he turned four. When the time came for them to take him back to surgery, he got scared. His mom, Barb, prayed with him and asked God to send his angels to watch over Jeremiah and keep him safe.

When her son woke up from the operation, Barb asked if he had seen the angels during the surgery. Jeremiah told her, "No, I just see'd Jesus. He holded my hands when the doctor fixed my eyes."

At the time, Barb had never heard of Colton Burpo or the story of his trip to heaven and back. But eighteen months later, she was reading *Heaven Is for Real,* and without telling Jeremiah anything about the book, she showed him Akiane's picture of Jesus and asked if he knew who it was.

Jeremiah replied matter-of-factly, "Yeah, that's Jesus. That's who held my hands when the doctor fixed my eyes."

It's been astonishing how many confirmations we've gotten that the man Colton identifies as Jesus—the man

Akiane saw from heaven and painted so beautifully—is the same man dozens of others have said they saw during similar experiences.

And not just kids but adults too. But because of their innocence, it's the kids' confirmations that seem so powerful. That's the genuine innocence I saw in Colton's face as he told me about his visit to heaven.

In the years since, I tried to absorb all he had told me about that visit and tried to imagine what he saw: Jesus' beard, his "pretty eyes," the "markers" on his hands and feet. But nothing prepared me for the *wow* moment when he saw Akiane's painting—and I saw him recognize a familiar face.

Suddenly, everything Colton had told me seemed to come into clearer focus. It all made sense.

Today, I want to assure you, this picture from Akiane is for real. Just like heaven is for real and God is for real. And I believe, based on the confirmations I've received, that although the picture was painted by a young child, it's pretty close to being accurate.

People ask me today, "Are you convinced that picture is really what Jesus looks like?"

In response, I ask them, "How much evidence do you need? How much does it take for God to convince you that something is right?"

For me, after millions of copies of *Heaven Is for Real* have been sold around the world, after hundreds of testimonies shared in person or by letter or e-mail, and by living with a boy who's a stickler for details, yes, I'm convinced. I have a copy of the picture hanging in my office, and I'm looking at it now. I believe I'm seeing the One who held my son on his lap in heaven.

Go to artnsoulwrks.com to see Prince of Peace:
The Resurrection, *Akiane's portrait of Jesus.*

*For now we see through a glass, darkly; but then
face to face: now I know in part; but then shall I
know even as also I am known.*

— 1 Corinthians 13:12 KJV

THIRTY-EIGHT

A Family Affair

Cassie, meanwhile, is the long-suffering older sister. This was demonstrated perfectly when we were all trying to think up a good title for this book.

I suggested Heaven by Four.

Sonja suggested Heaven, According to Colton.

Cassie suggested He's Back, but He's No Angel.

—*HEAVEN IS FOR REAL*, 154

Sonja

We've been asked many times since *Heaven Is for Real* was published how we keep our family's life "normal." They want to know if Cassie and Colby are jealous of the attention heaped on Colton since his story has spread around the world.

We tell them that Colton may get most of the attention when we're doing an interview or appearing at a speaking engagement somewhere, but when he's home with his family, he gets treated just like his siblings. His big sister Cassie is a hawk about that.

Not that Cassie has ever shown any jealousy about the attention focused on Colton outside the family. But she keeps Todd and me on our toes when it comes to making sure her younger brothers are held to the same expectations and rules we set for her when she was their age.

Todd and I understand. We're firstborn kids ourselves, and we know there's a tendency to "baby the baby" in a family. We work hard to be consistent in our parenting so that all three kids are treated the same. We knew Cassie would be watching carefully when Colton turned ten to see if we instituted the kids-do-their-own-laundry rule. And we did. In a few years she'll no doubt want to know that we enforce the same rules about dating and driving with the boys that we've established for her as she enters those years now.

In the Burpo household, there's a set of rules for everyone, and we do our best to enforce them equally. Yes, Colton may get to miss a little more school than the other two due to speaking engagements, but we work our tails off to arrange things so that we can give extra attention to the other two kids, one on one, when we get back from a trip.

When we're on the road as a family, it may be Colton who's onstage speaking and singing "Amazing Grace," but everyone has a job. Colby gets to come onstage and show audiences "this is what Colton looked like when he visited heaven." Then he works at his other job: handing out *Heaven Is for Real* bracelets.

Cassie's job is one she asked for. Like most public speakers, we have a merchandise table where our books are sold when we're speaking somewhere. Cassie was interested in that and enjoyed working at the table. In fact, now she *runs* the table when she travels with us. It's a big job for a fifteen-year-old, but she handles it like a pro.

One way I spend special time with my kids is to volunteer to be a class sponsor or to help chaperone school trips. Recently I spent four days accompanying Cassie and twenty-two other students to the state conference of the Future Business Leaders of America in Lincoln.

It meant a lot to Cassie that I took time off work and made that trip with her. How do I know? She told me so, both before and after the trip—even though she also told me she didn't want to ride in my car for the trip to Lincoln. It turned out that the sophomores were assigned to me, so she rode in the Burpo bus anyway, and it all turned out fine.

I loved seeing Cassie interact with her friends, and was proud of her for handling the pressure of competition so coolly. She didn't place in any of her events, and she was gracious about losing—which made me just as proud of her as if she had won.

I had just returned from a speaking trip to Florida the day before we left for the FBLA trip, and I had to rearrange my work schedule at the real estate office where I work. Cassie recognized what I had done so that I could go with her and her classmates on the trip. So when it was over and she told me, "Thanks, Mom," I knew she really meant it.

I like being with our kids and their friends, and I try to be fun to be with. Cassie told me she was glad I went with them. She said the other chaperones were "calm and nice."

I said, "So I'm the crazy one?"

She said, "Yeah, basically."

We encourage our kids to invite their friends to our house to hang out or to spend the night. I won't deny that it's a great way to be a fly on the wall and find out what's on their minds and what's going on in their lives.

Todd and I are like most parents we know: we're doing

the best we can to give our kids a solid foundation of love and direction while sharing our faith with them.

Todd

Every time I come into my office, I see a reminder that helps me keep in focus my responsibilities as a parent and pastor. Written in pencil in careful fifth-grader handwriting, it's a framed, essay Cassie wrote when she was ten years old. Here's what it says, misspelling and all:

My dad is my hero.
by Cassie Burpo

My dad, Todd Burpo, is my hero. He is a firefighter, pastor, and more. My dad is willing to help, caring about others, and a great person. My dad is there when I need help and when others need help too. He loves to help a lot.

My dad, being a firefighter, can be called anytime about a fire. My dad is a volunteer, so he doesn't get payed at all. He will go into a fire, risk his life, to save a person or animal in the fire. My dad and the other firefighters will put out a fire when needed. I am scared when my dad goes to a fire. He always has come back.

My dad is a pastor. He preaches about every Saturday night and Sunday morning. My dad talks about the right things all the time to people. When there is something needed done at the church he'll do it. He is dedicated at being a pastor.

It's true that Cassie, the big sister, is still making sure the house rules she grew up with are consistently enforced today for her two brothers. But her essay reminds me that she and her brothers—and a lot of other people too—are watching me and counting on me. And it provides as a daily reminder that even though she's about to turn sixteen, she still needs a hero. And that hero needs to be her dad.

So every day, amid all the other things I do and duties I fulfill, I want to make sure I can answer yes to the questions I ask myself:

Does Cassie know I still love her? Do I still make time for her? Set the right example for her? Can she look at me and be proud? And one day will she look for a man who might have some of the same qualities as her hero-dad to be her husband?

Even though I may be on the road, traveling a lot with Colton these days, as I write this I'm getting ready to pick up our jet skis from the shop and looking forward to the weekend when I can spend some time zipping around the lake with my daughter.

From the outside looking in, people seeing our family might assume Colton gets all the attention. But that's just not true.

The real truth is, all three of our kids are constantly watching Sonja and me for reassurance that we're parenting all of them consistently and also to see that we're being consistent in the way we live our lives, both inside our home and out in the world.

Cassie's essay is my daily reminder of that. When I walk into my office and see it there in its frame, I ask God to help

me be to Cassie and her brothers the kind of godly dad he
is to me—and to be the hero to Cassie that she thinks I am.

*One of the biggest principles of healthy
parenting is consistency. Would your household
pass a consistency check-up? If you need
to make improvements, God will help.*

*Train a child in the way he should go, and when he
is old he will not turn from it.*

—PROVERBS 22:6

THIRTY-NINE

Asking for and Giving Help

Another question people ask all the time is how Colton's experience has changed us. The first thing Sonja will tell you is that it absolutely broke us. See, pastors and their families are usually most comfortable in the role of "helper," not "helpee." Sonja and I had always been the ones who visited the sick, brought the meals, cared for others' kids, in times of need. We were adamantly self-reliant—maybe, in retrospect, to the point of being prideful. But that grueling stint in the hospital snapped our pride like a dry twig and taught us how to be humble enough to accept help from other people, physically, emotionally, and financially.

—HEAVEN IS FOR REAL, 153

Sonja

Todd and I are both firstborn, strong-willed, independent-minded, we-can-do-it-ourselves kind of people. We had lived in Imperial five years when Colton got sick, and during that time we had worked hard to serve the families in our church and to be good neighbors to those in need in our community.

It feels good to help someone in need. We all like to be the white knights in shining armor, showing up to rescue someone who needs a hot meal or a bag of groceries, a shoulder to cry on or a little relief from caring for kids or ailing family members. We don't like seeing people we know endure difficult situations, but we do like knowing that they know we're there for them when they need us.

It's easy to start feeling a little prideful when you're always the rescuer and never the rescued. I admit, there was some of that in Todd and me: the caring pastor and his caring wife showing up to save the day time and time again.

Then Todd broke his leg and couldn't work at the garage-door business we owned. Before he'd recovered from that crisis, he was laid up with kidney stones, followed by a cancer scare requiring a biopsy. Less than three months later, Colton's ordeal began, and by the time it was over, our bank account was drained and so were we. As the three-week-long nightmare unfolded, we hit bottom.

God broke our spiritual pride and our independence. He broke us mentally, spiritually, and financially. He broke us to the core. And in that humble, broken state, the helpers had to ask for help.

It came in the form of friends and compassionate strangers who surrounded us with love and care. Throughout our ordeal, including while we were with Colton in the hospital in North Platte, a ninety-minute drive away, friends in Imperial and North Platte cared for Cassie and got her to and from school and also drove her to North Platte to be with us in the hospital. They brought food, cleaned our house, did our laundry, and came to visit us in the hospital. Our family members spent their vacation to help us. Friends and family supported us with their prayers and helped us pay our bills. I can't imagine how we could have survived without these people who put aside their own schedules and needs to help us with ours.

Todd and I both had jobs back in Imperial, so we took turns staying with Colton in the hospital in North Platte, rushing back home to be with Cassie, and trying to keep up with our work back there. During that time there was never a day when we didn't have a hospital visitor. And let me tell you, we appreciated every one of them. They were people who understood that visiting the sick can be a greater gift to the sick person's family than to the one who is ill. To us, those kind friends were what I call "Jesus with skin on."

When it was my turn to stay with Colton, I was on round-the-clock "puke patrol," never leaving him alone for a second unless someone else was there. So I was especially grateful for those friends who came to visit. Sometimes I would ask the visitor to sit with Colton a few minutes just so I could use the bathroom!

One friend insisted I take a break and go downstairs to the hospital lobby. "I have your cell phone number. I'll call you if anything happens," she said.

I was amazed at the difference in my attitude and energy level after just a few minutes with a change of scenery.

We learned so much as we struggled through that nightmare, but one of the most important was that there is blessedness in brokenness. God uses broken people.

So many of those who helped us had been through diffi cult challenges themselves. When they shared their experience with us and told us we would get through our ordeal, their encouragement carried extra weight that gave us confidence.

We learned that sometimes what's needed most is simply for a friend to show up. You don't have to have profound words of comfort, quote Scripture or explain your theory on why God let the hard thing happen. Just be there. Go. If all you can do is cry with that friend, that's okay. Trust God to guide you in knowing what to do or say.

We know Satan uses people to hurt us, tear us down, but God uses people to build us up, to come alongside us and comfort us when we need it. Make it your goal to be those people he uses!

Now Todd and I are the broken people encouraging others, the ones who offer encouragement rooted in experience rather than platitudes. Now the help we give is based in humility rather than prideful independence.

The next time someone offers to help you or give you a gift, have the grace to receive their gift with a grateful heart. No excuses, no explanations, no, "Oh, no thanks. I'm fine. I don't need that." No, "I'll pay you back." Just say thank you. Let God use that person. Then let God use you. Be the answer to someone else's prayer. Start praying today about who you can give a gift to.

Do not grow weary in doing good.

—2 Thessalonians 3:13

FORTY

The Battle to Come

"There's going to be a war, and it's going to destroy this world. Jesus and the angels and the good people are going to fight against Satan and the monsters and the bad people. I saw it."

I thought of the battle described in the book of Revelation, and my heartbeat stepped up a notch. "How did you see that?"

"In heaven, the women and the children got to stand back and watch. So I stood back and watched." Strangely, his voice was sort of cheerful, as though he were talking about a good movie he'd seen. "But the men, they had to fight. And Dad, I watched you. You have to fight too."

—HEAVEN IS FOR REAL, 136

Todd

Colton says that when he was in heaven he watched as Jesus, the angels, and the "good people" battled "monsters . . . dragons and stuff" in a fierce battle for the world.

I know, I know. It sounds like we've moved out of the devotional reader category and headed off into the "fantasy" section of the bookstore. But what Colton saw is perfectly in sync with the book of Revelation, which describes the end of the world, including a fierce battle against dragons and other monsters, including locusts shaped like horses with men's faces, women's hair, lions' teeth, and tails like multi-stingered scorpions (Revelation 9:7–11).

Sounds like "dragons and stuff" to me.

I was amazed that Colton, who first described this scene to me when he was six years old, could describe it so matter-of-factly. I *wasn't* amazed that he had asked for a big sword so he could fight too. After all, with Jesus on his side, victory was assured. But one of the men fighting alongside Jesus in the battle apparently caught his eye. It was his dad.

Me.

Battling a monster.

And not with the bazooka, grenade launcher, M-16 rifle, Bradley tank, and nuclear warheads I would have hoped for but with a sword or a bow and arrow (two years after he'd witnessed the battle, Colton couldn't remember specifically what weapon I wielded).

I have to admit, I wasn't overly ecstatic to hear about this event waiting for me in the future. But then I realized that Colton had actually witnessed what I had learned long ago from studying Scripture and from my own experience here on earth: our enemy, Satan, is alive and well, and he threatens us every day in every way imaginable. The Bible says he "prowls around like a roaring lion looking for someone to devour" (1 Peter 5:8 NIV).

Who wrote that? Peter! You can hear in his words the

pain of being pounced on by that enemy. Today we're still in that fight that Peter knew firsthand. I personally fight it on a daily basis—but for now, it's a different kind of battle than one where I'm wielding a sword against monsters and dragons. Today, my battle seems to focus on two questions: Am I following Jesus like I should? And am I standing up for him like I should?

I think the biggest battle for most people is the second one. At least that's how it seems to me.

In today's world we get mixed messages about sharing our experiences and our faith. Some people want to hear, but most urge us to tone it down and keep our beliefs to ourselves. I'm amazed at how many people just don't want me to talk about the miracles I've seen. You've probably run into the same thing. There are even people who attend churches who say you can believe in Jesus any way you want, but just keep it to yourself. I strongly disagree, and I know God does too.

My faith, and Colton's faith, is based on a real God who has done real things for us. Real prayers have been answered, and real lives have been changed by a real God whose Son is Jesus. I know some people disagree; others may still be look-ing and questioning. I'm fine with that. But I'm not fine with *believers* not talking about what God has done for them.

I'm not saying we should be offensive in sharing our experiences. I'm not suggesting you stand on the street corner and preach to people waiting (eagerly) for the light to change. I'm just saying *stand*: Stand without wavering. Stand without apology. Stand confidently and say, "I know who Jesus is, and this is what he has done for me."

There's a passage in Acts 4 where Jesus' enemies

confronted the early believers. Their message was clear: If you just won't talk about Jesus, we'll leave you alone. You can believe what you want; just don't speak in his name anymore.

The same thing seems to be happening today. In our country we have abundant freedom when it comes to things like profanity and promiscuity but not when it comes to faith. Freedom of speech is in, and freedom of religion is on its way out in our country. Vulgarity and pornography? They're okay. Jesus? Not so much.

I know who's behind that position. You probably do too. He's the same one I'll be fighting against that day in Armageddon. If you want to fall before that enemy, all you have to do is keep your faith to yourself. Keep it quiet.

I know sometimes standing up for your faith might ruffle your friends' feathers. Praying before a meal might make other people in the restaurant uncomfortable. Reading a Bible in public might cause others to turn up their nose and walk away. When you stand up for your faith there are some times you won't feel popular or wanted. But at that point I have to ask you this question: which side are you on?

When the apostle Paul's life was coming to an end, he summed it up with this simple phrase: "I have fought the good fight." I think Paul said he was fighting the good fight because he knew which side he was on: the good side.

Colton had to remind me of that same fact when he was telling me about my fighting in the heavenly battle to come. Sometimes in the middle of the day-to-day issues we face here on earth, we forget the most important part of that battle, the final score. But just as Colton reminded me, let me now remind you of the best part: "Dad, Jesus wins."

I'm glad I'll fight on the winning side. How many of you will be joining me?

> *I challenge you to memorize 2 Timothy 4:7 and live in such a way that you, like Paul, can say this at the end of your life:*

I have fought the good fight, I have finished the race, I have kept the faith.

—2 Timothy 4:7

FORTY-ONE

Yes, No, and Not Yet

*"Hey Colton, I bet you asked if you could have a sword,
didn't you?" I said.*

*At that, Colton's scowl melted into a dejected frown,
and his shoulders slumped toward the floor. "Yeah, I did.
But Jesus wouldn't let me have one. He said I'd be too
dangerous."*

—HEAVEN IS FOR REAL, 133

Todd

Heaven is for real, and that means when a toddler visiting heaven asks Jesus for a real sword, Jesus says no. When Colton told me this, I had to wonder if Jesus knew a sword-wielding toddler would be too dangerous to himself—or to others.

This negative response in heaven came after Colton had gotten another no answer when he asked the angels to sing "We Will, We Will Rock You" as they escorted him to Jesus. And then there was the issue of his sister hugging him—when being hugged by a girl wasn't this little guy's favorite thing.

We may think of heaven as a place where we get everything we want, where we always get our way. But that wouldn't be *real*. Heaven is a good and perfect place, but sometimes what we think we want, at least here on earth, doesn't meet heaven's good-and-perfect criteria. Sometimes Jesus says no.

When I'm honest with myself and really look at what's happening, I realize that most of the time when I get a no answer to my prayers, I'm praying for *easy*. On those days when I ask God to make my life easy, I tend to hear lots of nos as the challenges roll in.

No is not my favorite answer, for sure. But I've lived long enough now and have had enough glimpses of God's bigger plan for my life that I can see God at work in many of those negative answers. I have to agree with the message in Garth Brooks' song "One of God's Greatest Gifts Is Unanswered Prayers."

Sometimes God says no, sometimes he says yes, and I can handle both of those answers. But let me tell you what's harder for me than no. It's when God says, "Wait." It's the "not yet" answers that are hardest for me. The *wait* answers. The answers that seem like no answer at all for a long time.

I am, by nature, a let's-get-things-done kind of guy. Let's go. Let's do it. Let's make it happen. For me, waiting is difficult. So I tend to ask God, "If you want this, and surely you do, why not *now*? Why can't you make it happen *today*?"

Then God whispers something like this to me: *You're a parent. You know how this works.*

If my three-year-old son were to have asked me for a

sharp sword, there's no way I would have given it to him. I would know he couldn't handle it yet.

Right now I'm struggling with another stage of life as a parent. I have a teenager who will soon turn sixteen. Almost every parent knows what that means: "Dad, can I have the keys?"

Fortunately there are some laws in our society I really appreciate during this stage. One of them is that before someone sits behind the wheel of a moving vehicle he or she has to pass a test that hopefully demonstrates that person can operate the vehicle carefully, safely, and courteously— and come back home to Mom and Dad in one piece. Until teenagers are ready, that law helps us parents say, "You have to wait."

To teenagers eager to drive and have the freedom to go where they please, that wait can seem like an eternity. But for their sake especially, and for other people's sakes too, a parent can't let kids drive until they're ready. So they have to wait. And grow. And learn. And eventually they get their driver's license.

Then, after sixteen, life continues, and they keep growing and maturing. For me, there was a growing period before I was ready to become a husband. I needed to wait and add some more knowledge and maturity to my lifetime collection. Then, after marriage, there was another growing period before I was ready to become a father. Those gifts I now enjoy, my marriage and my children, God gave to me. But I had to wait until he knew I was ready for them.

In the book of Genesis, we watch a young man named Joseph grow and gain maturity. Joseph had an incredible gift of seeing and interpreting dreams. But like most teenagers, when he first discovered the gift, he wasn't mature enough to handle it. His arrogance caused him to boast to his brothers and even to his parents that he'd had a dream that said one day they would bow down to him.

Well, that arrogance led to a lot of awful events in Joseph's life: Betrayal. Slavery. A dungeon. Then, after a long wait, the second-highest position in Egypt.

Finally, seventeen years after that first dream he'd boasted about, it came true: Joseph's brothers bowed before him asking for food.

If an immature person had been in that place, he could have gloated over his brothers' forced humility. He could have mocked them, punished them. Instead, this is what Joseph said about his brothers selling him into slavery: "You meant evil against me, but God meant it for good" (Genesis 50:20).

It's almost like he was saying, "I needed to grow up, and God used the difficulties you caused me to suffer to make that happen. Those difficulties brought me to this point where I am mature enough to handle the dream God gave me."

Now, I'm not saying immaturity is the only reason God gives us not-yet answers to our prayers. But in my life, it's been a big reason why I've had to wait. I see that now, after the growing has been done, the waiting is over, and the prayer has been answered.

Could there be some answer to your prayer where the obstacle to *yes* is a growth issue? Here are two truths to remember if a growth issue *is* causing you to have to wait: First, God will know when you're ready—before you know. And second, if you ask him to grow you so you *can* be ready, he's pretty good at that too.

*What can God say yes to tomorrow
if you grow today?*

*I waited patiently for the LORD; and he inclined
unto me, and heard my cry.*

—PSALM 40:1 KJV

FORTY-TWO

Being Ourselves in Heaven

With what Colton had said about Pop and about his sister, I began to think about heaven in a different way. Not just a place with jeweled gates, shining rivers, and streets of gold, but a realm of joy and fellowship, both for those who are with us in eternity and those still on earth, whose arrival we eagerly anticipated. A place where I would one day walk and talk with my grandfather who had meant so much to me, and with the daughter I had never met.

—*Heaven Is for Real,* 103

Todd

Many of Colton's stories about heaven have convinced me that we'll retain our identities there—our quirks, our preferences, our uniqueness. But we will lose the bad stuff—our selfishness, our insecurities, our guilt, sicknesses and disabilities. Even though our heavenly bodies will definitely be better, we'll still be *us*. And so will our family members. But they may not be as we remembered them. That's why I suggest you keep that box of old family photos next to your bed.

Let me explain.

As a firefighter, I've seen a lot of house fires, and let me tell you, they rarely happen like you see in the movies. In real life, family members, and even firefighters, don't have time to develop a dramatic story line while flames roar around them. In real life, you have about five survivable minutes to get out of that house before deadly smoke and toxic fumes overwhelm you. In real life, you may have only ten minutes until the roof collapses. Some modern construction methods can make newer houses far more dangerous than older ones.

You don't have time to run around looking for your most valuable possessions. You and your family members need to know exactly what you will do when that smoke alarm goes off in the middle of the night (or in the daytime, for that matter). Get the people and get out!

But if you have time to grab maybe one thing besides the people, let me suggest something you might keep close to the bed so you can take it along. What I'm suggesting you take with you out of the fire is that box or album of old photos your mother or grandmother may have given you. You know the one I'm talking about—the box hidden in the back of a closet shelf right now. The box holding that picture of Grandma and Grandpa on their wedding day. The one of your great-granddad the day he went off to war. The pictures that show the previous generations of your family not as they may appear now but as they looked in their prime. Take those photos with you out of the fire.

Why? Because they'll help you recognize the people who are going to come to greet you when you get to heaven.

As Sonja and I travel the country, we're asked again and again, "Are we still going to be ourselves in heaven?" and, "How will I recognize my loved ones when I get to heaven?"

Colton's experiences convince us the answer to the first question is definitely *yes*. The answer to the second question may depend on whether you've studied those old family pictures. Because those who died when they were old or crippled by illness or injury aren't going to be old or crippled when you see them in heaven. Won't it be fun to call them by name rather than being like Colton and have to have the relationships explained to you?

It's not only Colton's experiences that convince me we'll retain our identities in heaven. I also base that opinion on the glimpse of heaven the Bible gives us in Matthew 17 when it describes two early Bible characters, Elijah and Moses, who came back to earth as themselves with the same names. While they chatted with Jesus, the apostles Peter, James, and John got to see them and were introduced to them as the same Moses and Elijah whose stories had been told in the Old Testament. They were in their heavenly bodies, and yet there they were on earth, named and recognizable.

When we get to heaven, we will retain our individuality. Our heavenly bodies will be just as diverse as our earthly ones. After all, God didn't use a cookie-cutter when he made us. God loves individuality and creativity.

But how many of you know that God also loves families? Our relationships with one another, even though they will be better, will still be intact as well. When Colton visited heaven, he was a little boy who still needed to be looked after, and his great-grandfather, Pop, was one of those who did that. After hearing Colton's story, and having him say that his great-grandfather, Pop, was looking out for him and his sister there, many people who have lost a parent and a child have told us how comforting that thought is—to know that their mom or dad is watching out for their son or daughter in heaven.

It's another reason that so many people have been impacted by *Heaven Is for Real*. All of us who believe in heaven have had that hope; Colton's visit helps confirm it for us.

Interestingly, our family members in heaven recognized Colton before he recognized them. That fact has sent me digging through our own box of old black-and-white photos, studying those faces of my grandparents, great-grandparents, aunts and uncles as they looked in their younger days. When I get to heaven, I want to recognize those loved ones, including those I never even met, and call them by name as they come up to greet me. That makes those old pictures pretty valuable to me. That's why I suggest they be something you take with you out of a burning house.

Just let me add one more thought. What if your house never catches on fire? Fire or no fire, don't you think it would still be worth your time to sit down with your kids and study those old pictures anyway? Then, unlike Colton, you or your child may not be surprised when you get to heaven and an unknown little girl, or some other bright-faced person, eager to greet you, comes running up to give you a big hug.

*As far as stuff is concerned, is there
anything else in your house today that will
matter to you when you get to heaven,
besides the people in those pictures?*

*His family will go on forever. His kingdom
will last before me like the sun. It will continue
forever, like the moon, like a dependable witness
in the sky.*

—Psalm 89:36–37 NCV

Heaven Changes Everything

"Oh good!" [Colton] said. "That means I get to go back to heaven!"

—*HEAVEN IS FOR REAL,* 113

Sonja

Maybe nothing describes how heaven changes everything more than what happened when Todd showed Colton, then about five, a bunny lying dead on the pavement. Colton had a bad habit of pulling away from us and zipping away without looking where he was going. He'd almost run into the street a couple of times, and when it happened again that day, Todd grabbed him at the edge of the curb and showed him the dead rabbit a few feet away. "That's what can happen if you run out and a car doesn't see you!" he told Colton. "You could not only get hurt; you could die!"

We were two years past Colton's heavenly visit, but the experience hadn't lost one bit of its appeal for him. He looked up at Todd and grinned. "Oh, good!" he said. "That means I get to go back to heaven!"

Imagine being completely fearless on earth because you know that after this life you're going to heaven—and you know, *really know*, you're going to love it there. That's the promise heaven holds for us. That's how it changes everything. Whatever situation you're going through right now, keep that promise in mind.

Knowing God has prepared a place for us reminds us of how our kids' anticipation builds before their birthdays. Most likely they've asked for something specific, something they really, really, reeeeeeally want, as our younger son Colby might say.

We listen, considering their request without any sign of commitment. But often, all the time they're talking about that item they reeeeeeally want, we know it's already bought and paid for, wrapped and hidden away somewhere. In our minds, the gift is already theirs, but they don't know that. They haven't seen it yet. They're hoping for it, but until they see it, it won't seem real.

That's heaven. It's God's incredible gift, and it's waiting for us.

Todd

I long for heaven and often wish I could get there sooner rather than later. Sometimes I even dream about it.

When you long for something, it impacts all of the details of your life. It's like when you've saved up your money for a wonderful trip—maybe it's an overseas cruise or a monthlong stay in the place of your dreams. Whatever the destination, let's say it's the trip of a lifetime. Most of us wouldn't be able to plan that kind of trip by ourselves. We would need a travel agent, someone who had been there and could tell us what to expect and how to prepare for it.

A good travel agent provides literature that shows you what your destination looks like, how the people dress and what their customs are. He or she might even have a contact person waiting for you who will meet your flight and help you get to your lodging, pointing out scenic and historic sites along the way. A travel agent makes it easier to imagine what you have to look forward to. And the more you picture that wonderful destination the more eager you become to get there.

That's how I feel now about heaven. It took me awhile to realize, when our story began, that we had been given a heavenly travel agent, one who could give us an insider's view of what awaits us at our *real* final destination. The more Colton told us, the more my eagerness grew.

And now, boy, do I want to go! No doubt about it, I'm ready. And unlike earthly trips, this is one trip I'm 100 percent sure I'm going to make!

My longing for heaven saturates everything I do. It has caused my priorities to shift and helped replace the worries and trials I encounter each day with thoughts of the wonderful, carefree place I'll be living in the future.

Looking forward to heaven is like that—but so much bigger. When you're heaven-minded and have that kind of eager anticipation, all kinds of things will change in your life. You'll find healing as you release hurts and pains that others can't let go of. You might not have the answers to all of your present-day issues and challenges, but you know that one day you will get those answers in heaven.

When you're heaven-minded you also find fulfillment. When others live without any direction or meaning in this world, you live with the confidence that your life has found its course and your bearings are set. You know your destination is heaven.

With a heavenly mind-set you'll find hope at the funeral of friends and family. While you're joining others in mourning the loved one's death because you will miss him or her, you'll also be picturing the joy that person is experiencing in heaven as he or she reconnects with beloved family members already there. You'll be happy knowing that person is seeing God face-to-face, and you'll know without a doubt that you'll see your loved one again.

When you're heaven-minded, the only thing that matters here, in the long run, is what—or who—you take with you. Who else is going to be there because of the boldness, confidence, peace, and fulfillment you've shown as you lived a heaven-minded life on earth?

We can't send Colton to your home to be your own heavenly travel agent, but we've written *Heaven Is for Real* and now *Heaven Changes Everything* to provide the kind of appealing information and accurate descriptions a good travel agent would share with you. Our prayer is that we've ignited in your heart the same fire of enthusiasm we feel in ours as we eagerly look forward to making heaven our eternal home.

We want you to know, above everything else, that *heaven* is God's last word. Here on earth we may define ourselves by our struggles and our failures, our problems and our fears, but if you love Jesus, those difficulties are momentary setbacks. They're not the last word.

A bitter divorce? It's not the last word!

Cancer? It's not the last word!

Grief? If you and your dear ones love Jesus, grief is not the last word.

For these reasons and so many others, my mind's default setting now seems to be heaven and what it's going to be like there. The images can be very powerful. Recently I was driving somewhere when the song "I Can Only Imagine" by MercyMe came on the radio, and I almost stopped the car in the middle of the highway, so strong was the image that came to me, prompted by an incident that had happened when I had first asked Colton about the song several years ago.

The songwriter ponders what his reaction will be when he first meets Jesus in heaven. On that particular day I realized my son knew the answer. I immediately went home and asked Colton about the lyrics. I don't remember exactly how I asked him, but I absolutely remember his answer. I told him I'd heard a song that tried to imagine what someone would do the first time he or she saw Jesus. Colton, then four years old, said, "Oh, Dad, that's easy." Then he dropped to his knees, put his forehead to the ground, and stretched his short arms out in front of him—a kneeling posture that, as far as I knew, he had never seen in any Sunday school class or church service. Then he popped back up and said earnestly, "Dad, that's exactly what you do when you see Jesus."

The memory still takes my breath away—and has the potential for middle-of-the-road traffic jams. It also adds to the eagerness I feel as I anticipate my arrival in heaven. I love thinking about being so glad, and so grateful, to see Jesus that I spontaneously fall down on my knees before him.

And I know he'll be glad to see me. In fact, he's been

praying that I would join him there. He's praying you'll join him there too. Please don't disappoint him. He's waiting for you in heaven. And that changes everything.

Listen to MercyMe's song "I Can Only Imagine"—and imagine yourself following Colton's lead in how you respond when you see Jesus for the first time.

Father, I want those you have given me to be with me where I am, and to see my glory, the glory you have given me because you loved me before the creation of the world.

—JOHN 17:24 NIV

COLTON'S PRAYER FOR YOU

Earlier in this book we mentioned a spontaneous prayer that Colton prayed at the end of an interview with Trinity Broadcasting Network in the fall of 2011. Because we feel it is so vital—not only to the message of this book but also to the message from heaven that Colton has delivered to us all—we have repeated it here. Was Colton praying for you?

Dear Father God,

I just hope all those people out there who haven't found you yet, or need to be reinforced by your Word, Lord, just please help them so that they may be able to come closer to you, so that one day they may receive the gift that you have given them. And Lord, I wish that, even though we have a lot of people out there who might not believe this, I just hope you bless them so then they will figure out that you are real, you are God. In Jesus' name. Amen.

ABOUT THE AUTHORS

Todd Burpo is the pastor of Crossroads Wesleyan Church in Imperial, Nebraska (population: 2,071). He travels and speaks internationally with HIFR Ministries and also continues to serve Imperial on the local volunteer fire department. He is also the chaplain for the Nebraska State Volunteer Firefighters' Association. Todd graduated summa cum laude from Oklahoma Wesleyan University in 1991 with a BA in theology and was ordained in 1994 by the Wesleyan Church.

Sonja Burpo is a busy mom to Cassie, Colton, and Colby and works as a real estate office manager. Sonja also travels and speaks for audiences with HIFR Ministries. With a BS in elementary education from Oklahoma Wesleyan University and a master's in library and information science, Sonja is a certified teacher in the state of Nebraska. She has taught in the public school system both in Oklahoma as well as in Imperial. Sonja is passionate about children's ministry and continues to teach children at Crossroads Wesleyan Church.

www.heavenisforreal.net
www.hifrministries.org